CW00481755

Rich Forever

*What They Didn't Teach You about Money,
Finance and Investments in School*

BIANCA MILLER-COLE
AND DR BYRON COLE

JOHN MURRAY

First published in Great Britain by John Murray One in 2023
An imprint of John Murray Press

1

A CIP catalogue record for this title is available from the British Library

Hardback ISBN 978 1 399 80759 3
ebook ISBN 978 1 399 80761 6

Typeset by KnowledgeWorks Global Ltd.

Printed and bound in Great Britain by Clays Ltd, Elcograf S.p.A.

John Murray Press policy is to use papers that are natural, renewable and recyclable products and made from wood grown in sustainable forests. The logging and manufacturing processes are expected to conform to the environmental regulations of the country of origin.

John Murray Press
Carmelite House
50 Victoria Embankment
London EC4Y 0DZ

www.johnmurraypress.co.uk

John Murray Press, part of Hodder & Stoughton Limited
An Hachette UK company

Contents

About the Authors

Dr Byron Cole

Byron is multi-award-winning entrepreneur, author and business start-up expert with a diverse portfolio of over 21 businesses spanning the UK and UAE.

As a business mentor, he has had the privilege of guiding countless individuals towards success, generating millions of pounds for his mentees.

His published works include *Self Made*, a comprehensive guide covering the entire business development process, from start-up to exit. It offers practical and implementable advice. Additionally, *The Business Survival Kit*, achieved *Sunday Times* bestselling status in the UK.

In 2022, Byron's dedication and contributions to entrepreneurship were recognised by the University of Greenwich, where he was honoured with an honorary degree. This recognition further validates his commitment to excellence and reinforces his status as a prominent figure in the entrepreneurial realm.

Bianca Miller-Cole

Bianca Miller-Cole is an award-winning entrepreneur, workshop facilitator and internationally renowned professional speaker.

In 2014, Bianca was the runner-up on The Apprentice, the BBC television series in which candidates compete in front of millions of viewers to go into business partnership with multi-millionaire tycoon, Lord Sugar. Bianca is the founder of go to personal branding company The Be Group and her retail brand, Bianca Miller London. Since writing bestselling book *Self Made* Bianca has mentored over 1,000 entrepreneurs to assist them in scaling their business to 6–7 figures. She is an in-demand public speaker, non-executive director and was awarded a Power Profile by LinkedIn in 2016 and the Forbes 30 under 30 list in 2018.

Acknowledgements

We would like to thank our families; our Self-Made mentoring community who have provided us with enormous love and support; our interviewees – Ella Weinburg, Andrea Richards, Aldred Zadey, Debodun Osekita and Marine Tanguy – all of them renowned industry experts; we would also like to thank Jonathan and the team for giving us this platform to transform lives. And finally, thanks to Trevor and Everyone who helped put this book together.

Byron:

I would like to give thanks to God.

And a big shout out to my amazing wife, co-author, co-investor and business partner, Bianca. You inspire me daily.

This book is to help everyone create a better life for themselves and their families. Enjoy.

Byron (I live to transform lives)

Bianca:

Byron, to be writing our third book as we build our romantic, financial and business lives together is nothing short of a dream come true. We have built a life to be proud of but moreover we have used our experiences to help others and for me that is our legacy.

To my mum, dad, family and friends for always being my biggest cheerleaders every step I take and for every new venture.

And for my clients and mentees who inspire me daily to keep learning so I can share those lessons to help others. And of course my clients who have enabled me to grow a business that has given me the revenue to experience much of what has been described in this book – thank you.

Foreword

In the ever-evolving landscape of finance and economics, we find ourselves navigating a terrain fraught with complexities and uncertainties. Money, once relegated to the hushed corners of conversation, now commands the spotlight as a central force shaping our lives, aspirations, and futures. The dawn of the entrepreneur (and intrapreneur), the digital age, and the rise of transformative technologies have conspired to place money at the epicentre of our existence. As the world shifts, we must equip ourselves with the knowledge and wisdom to comprehend and harness this powerful force.

Rich Forever: What They Didn't Teach You about Money, Finance and Investments in School arrives as a beacon of light in the midst of this financial maze. Bianca Miller-Cole and Dr Byron Cole have masterfully crafted a compass to navigate the uncharted waters of wealth, presenting insights that would be invaluable to any journey.

As a staunch advocate for the equitable redistribution of wealth, the cultivation of legacy, and the nurturing of generational prosperity, I have dedicated my life to fostering a world where wealth serves not only the fortunate few but reaches the hands of all who seek to elevate their circumstances. I believe that true wealth transcends mere accumulation; it lies in our ability to enrich every facet of our lives and others – be it in health, love, relationships, philanthropy or financial stability – in this way we should all strive to be 'Rich Forever'.

This book embraces a holistic approach to wealth, addressing not just financial acumen, but also the profound connections between personal well-being, relationships, and our financial path. It's an acknowledgement that true wealth is not solely measured by numbers, but by the impact we create, the lives we touch, and the lasting legacy we leave behind.

In these pages, Bianca and Byron offer a blueprint for navigating the intricate landscape of money, finance, and investments. Their insights stem from both their personal triumphs and tribulations, serving as a testament to the fact that prosperity is within the grasp of every individual willing to seek knowledge and take action.

As you delve into the pages of *Rich Forever*, you will find a treasure trove of wisdom that can change the trajectory of your financial journey. Bianca and Byron have brilliantly woven together insights on money, investments, and finance with timeless principles that embrace the profound connection between wealth and holistic well-being. With practical advice on saving, investing, and making sound financial decisions, this book demystifies the once elusive world of finance. It empowers readers to make informed choices, transcending the cycle of financial uncertainty that plagues so many.

It is with great pleasure that I endorse this book, for it encapsulates the very essence of the ideals I have dedicated my life to. May this work serve as a guiding light, illuminating your path towards a future rich not only in monetary success but also in the intangible riches that truly define a life well-lived.

Kabir Mulchandani
Founder of FIVE Holdings
Billionaire Philanthropist

Introduction

Something unusual has happened over the past few years. Money is being widely and openly discussed.

Why is that surprising? Well, the truth is that money used to be a topic that a lot of people steered well clear of, perhaps considering it inappropriate, or simply too personal, to discuss with friends or even family.

Lately, however, there has been a sea change in attitudes, for both positive and negative reasons.

On the plus side, programmes such as *Dragons' Den* – and its US equivalent, *Shark Tank* – have highlighted the work of entrepreneurs and investors. This has in turn created huge interest in entrepreneurship, leading increasing numbers of people to start their own businesses. And for those seeking inspiration, business success stories are a staple of newspapers, magazines and the internet.

There are also a great many investment-focused success stories. In recent years, we've heard a lot about the money that can be made from investing in cryptocurrencies or their closely related siblings, NFTs (non-fungible tokens). There is, of course, huge interest in longer-established options such as property or shares.

But if there's interest in making money, there are also some very real concerns about maintaining a standard of living in a time of unprecedented economic turbulence.

A lot has changed in recent times. For many people, work has become more precarious, meaning that the concept of a job for life with a pension from an employer who looks after you is no longer a reality for most people. These days, you have to plan your finances and make your own financial arrangements. Financial security is no longer a given.

Then there is a growing sense that things are broken. The great financial crisis of the late 2000s raised the uncomfortable proposition that the world's banking system was not as stable as everyone – including governments – had assumed.

More recently, the pandemic disrupted the world's economy and the war in Ukraine has caused oil, gas and food prices to jump to levels that challenge the ability of many people to simply make ends meet. In many countries, there is a cost-of-living crisis. Having enough money is not a nice-to-have but a vital concern for increasing numbers of people.

As we write this book, there is the expectation that inflation – the rate that prices rise year-on-year – will continue to stay high and that a recession is imminent.

So now is a very good time to talk about money.

Everyone has questions

And almost everyone has questions. How can I manage my finances more effectively? How can I preserve what I've got? How can I make my money work harder for me?

We've heard a lot of these questions over the past year or so. Following the publication of our previous two books – *Self Made* and *The Business Survival Kit* – we built a community of people with a strong interest in making the most of their lives through following and executing their ambitions. Given the turbulence of the last few years, it isn't surprising that many of the people we speak to are seeking to build a stable financial foundation for themselves against a backdrop of economic uncertainty.

Too much confusion

And what they find is that the world of money often seems to be confusing. There's a lot of jargon, a lot of apparent complexity and many misconceptions. When you break it all down, money isn't really that complicated, but financial education is very poor. Most schools don't provide much help with financial management. Their students go out into the world ill-prepared. Sometimes they make mistakes which can have consequences for years to come.

And that's partly why we've written this book. Drawing on our experience, our intention is to provide a roadmap for preserving and growing wealth through good money management and investment. To do that we have drawn on our own experiences and financial journeys. In addition, we'll be tapping into the knowledge of some renowned financial experts.

But that's just part of our ambition. We don't simply aim to help you get by. We want to provide the information that will help you master money and make it work to serve your own ambitions. To put it simply, we want you to become as rich as you can possibly be and stay that way.

We are businesspeople and investors. So, in that respect, money is the product of what we do. We understand how it works.

But we weren't always in business. Our financial stories began when we were children and extended into young adulthood. As we encountered the world, we had to learn about money.

So just for a moment, let's take the time to tell you about our individual journeys and how they've shaped our approach to money.

Byron's story

So, at this point, the question I hear you ask is: 'How do you guys know so much about money, finance and credit?' Well, it's something I've been keenly interested in from a very young age.

Why? Well, I grew up on one of Europe's largest council estates (commonly referred to in the USA as projects or colloquially as 'the hood') where aspiration was low – people didn't even know lack of aspiration was a problem; that was just where they lived. Everyone struggled to get by, and some people didn't even make it. In this environment I saw things I wouldn't wish on my worst enemy and yet I pursued my thirst for disposable income and that fuelled my early entrepreneurial hustles, which ranged from buying and selling CDs to buying and selling cars. I always wanted to know what I could do to make more money. I completed my school education having failed my GCSEs and had to start again at college, this time focusing on learning and entrepreneurship. I made a hobby of trawling through government websites and sourcing opportunities. Growing up in a single-parent family, with a sister as a quadruple amputee, I knew I wanted more for them and would strive to make a change for my family.

My keen interest in finance continued into the workplace. As a young man, I worked at a sportswear retail brand known as First Sport. The company offered a proprietary card – essentially providing credit to customers – but quite a few applicants were turned down. I became interested in why some people were refused.

Moving on from there, I worked at British mobile phone retailer Phones4U as a sales assistant. Customers were required to have good credit in order for them to get a mobile phone. This created a bit of a challenge for me. I was on commission, so it was in my personal interest to get sales over the line. It did me no good at all if a customer came in with the intention of buying a new phone, only to be refused because his or her credit wasn't good enough. I wanted to understand why some customers would get offered a few phones and some none.

Actually, I went further than that. I started working with clients to try and help them resolve their creditworthiness issues because sometimes it was just something very simple and silly on their file.

I was 18 years of age. I didn't get paid any extra for working outside of the remit of my normal job but I was hungry for the sales, so I made sure I understood credit inside out and outside in. I did the research, and when customers were turned down, I invited them to bring in their credit reports. We went through the reports and worked out ways and means to build a better score.

At university I began to research the property market. To be honest, I was obsessed with a UK TV show called *Homes under the Hammer* and I don't really know why. It was all about buying properties at auction either to resell them or rent them out to tenants. I began to go to auction houses – really, I had no business being there – and after a while, the professionals got to know me. They would take me out to sites and show me how properties were bought, sold and renovated.

The turning point came when I was offered an opportunity to sell some of the properties I was looking at. There were no buyers in my personal network so I went to upmarket hotels and I spoke to anyone who would listen to me. I became very good at selling in this way, and by the age of 21 I had earned enough money to buy my own property. I was a landlord.

That led to me investing in an estate agency, and my knowledge of finance extended from credit and property to running a business. Today, I am a successful businessman, I have a portfolio of properties and an extensive investment portfolio, I bank with Coutts & Co. (the bank the Royal Family uses) and have a triple 999 credit score, which happens to be the top rating on credit agency Experian (we will share how to achieve this later). I believe that, while I was born poor, I will die rich.

And that's an important point. If you are born poor, that's not your fault. But you needn't be poor when you are older. You have resources, information and opportunities around you. If you don't take advantage of them, then that's something you have to take responsibility for.

It isn't always easy. When I went through my journey, I had nobody to hold my hand or show me the ropes. It doesn't have to be that way; we want to share everything we have learned to help you to understand personal finance. Because money matters and we should all be aiming to be rich forever.

Everything that we talk about today in this book I've experienced or worked with clients very closely to help them achieve. And I want to help *you* succeed. I would like everyone to have 'Byron problems'. Which car do I drive today – the Rolls-Royce or the Bentley? The frustration of being out in a car that doesn't have a massage seat. Having to cope when a housekeeper is on holiday. These are all the 'problems' associated with doing well and we want 'Byron problems' for all of our readers.

Byron problems

Let's try a thought experiment. Take out a piece of paper and write down your name followed by the word 'problems'.

Now write down a list of problems that you would really like to have this year. No, this isn't an opportunity to reflect on life's difficulties. Instead focus on the small 'problems' and frustrations that that stem from being successful.

Bianca's story

 I grew up in an entrepreneurial environment. My dad had a number of businesses, from property to luxury kitchens. My mum was a freelance make-up artist in television and media.

Neither worked nine to five. They would work long hours. And as all entrepreneurs have experienced, they had *great* months and *bad* months, and they always worked very hard, sometimes just to make ends meet.

I have also always had a keen interest in money. You can track that right back to my first entrepreneurial pursuit at the age of four. I set up an art store in my bedroom – trading pieces of 'art' (I was no Picasso) for money. My parents would buy the pieces, so my piggy bank was full. Later – at the much more advanced age of 12 – I set up a dance agency. A local primary school needed something to occupy their students after hours. I got a couple of my friends to give dance lessons. I would invoice the school, pay my friends and take a mark-up. Profit was very important.

At 17, I started an events production company for under-18s. We managed to do about three events, before my parents told me, 'Stop trying to make money and concentrate on your education.' They had invested in me by giving me a private education in the hope that there would be a constant evolution and generational improvements. Their investment was not lost on me.

I did all of this while having a retail job in a sports store on a Saturday and pocket money provided by my family. So, as you can see, I was always keen on money! My parents and grandparents used to laugh about giving me cash on birthdays. It went straight into my savings; I was not in the habit of spending my own money unless I *really* needed to. Because I had saved, I was able to buy a car and pay for all the running and maintenance costs including the ridiculous insurance premiums paid by young drivers.

Fast-forward to my university days. I applied for a 'maintenance loan', and I put the funds into a National Savings and Individual Savings Accounts (ISAs) and bonds. Meanwhile, I worked on the weekends to pay for my 'maintenance' costs, I took a loan for my tuition fees, and I was privileged to have my parents pay for my accommodation. My money management resulted in my keen interest in my credit score during my student years, which meant that, when I applied for my first credit card with an excellent credit score, I was offered a platinum card with a significant limit. From that point, I was hooked. I wanted to know exactly how I could increase and maintain that score.

When I secured a corporate job, my expenditure changed but my obsession with saving and sourcing financial tips to improve my opportunities did not.

I was still scouring the internet for tips and tricks, many of which were trial and error, but I was gaining knowledge. That enabled me to become a trusted adviser for friends and family alike, many of whom were not as financially savvy. My savings enabled me to purchase my first property at 23 (with Byron), and I have not looked back since.

Today, I am still a saver, but there is a difference. I am not only a saver but also an investor and a money maker. All three sit comfortably together. I want to make money but I also want it to work for me.

But here's what is important. Saving, investment, wealth creation – all these things can help you build a better life for yourself (and your loved ones), but you need to know how the system works.

For instance, if asked, most people can think of a hundred ways to spend their money, but could they deliver a list as lengthy for saving it and making it work for them? And I'm not saying that as an implied criticism. Sometimes people simply don't know what to do.

Should it be so hard to get the information that we all need? Indeed, information that we should really have been told at a young age, before we make mistakes that become inscribed in our credit history and affect our ability to manage money well. I don't think so.

And again, this speaks to the purpose of this book. It isn't just for those who have made mistakes. It is for those who are nervous about what to do with their money. To this day, I am still very cautious with my money. Unlike Byron, I continue to be fairly risk-averse and require extensive research to make a decision. In that respect, this book is for you but it is also for me.

We conceived, researched and planned *Rich Forever* together and collaboratively but divided up the writing of individual chapters according to our expertise, experience and interests. You can identify the author by the sketch beside the chapter heading or section.

What does it mean to be rich?

So let's return to the theme of our book. We want you to be rich forever, but what does that mean? To some extent wealth is relative.

But here's a definition. We think there are three levels to wealth – layers that you move through:

1 **Financial stability:** This level of wealth is characterized by having enough money to cover basic living expenses, such as housing, food and transportation, without worrying about living pay check to pay check. Financial stability allows individuals to save for emergencies and plan for the future

2 **Financial security:** Financial security is a higher level of wealth, characterized by having enough money to cover all living expenses comfortably, including discretionary spending and investments. Financial security allows individuals to feel confident in their financial future and pursue their goals and dreams.

3 **Financial independence:** Financial independence is the highest level of wealth, characterized by having enough money to cover all living expenses and achieve financial goals without relying on earned income. Financial independence allows individuals to have more control over their time and pursue their passions, hobbies and interests without worrying about money.

But there are also different ways to be rich:

- rich financially (asset rich or cash rich)
- rich in love
- rich in time
- rich in health
- rich in opportunity.

This book will take you on a journey to work on your financial riches and wealth planning, which in turn will impact many of the other aspects of building a rich life.

What you will learn in this book

In this book, we'll tell you:

- how money works
- how to identify and take advantage of investment opportunities
- how to maintain a good credit rating – an essential in the modern world
- how to set goals
- how to plan your finances, not just for you but to leave a legacy for your family.

Through our eyes and those of experts, we'll take you on a comprehensive journey and help you understand how to make your money work as hard for you as you have worked to earn it.

And, ultimately, this book may help you on your way towards financial freedom. A situation where you no longer have to work day-to-day and earn a salary in order to afford the lifestyle you want.

This book is for you if:

- You are in a financial pickle and want to understand clear frameworks that can help you get out.
- You feel the education system and your family did not prepare you for the trappings of adulthood.
- You recognize you are living for instant gratification but want to be more future focused.
- You didn't come from a wealthy family but would like a wealthy family to come from you.
- You want to focus on your long-term wealth.
- You want to provide wealth not just for yourself but for future generations.

Throughout your journey with this book, we would love to hear from you: if it alters your mindset, post and tag us; if it alters your financial status, post and tag us; if it changes your legacy, post and tag us; even if it just improves your credit score, post and tag us.

@mrbselfmade (Instagram and TikTok) – Dr Byron Cole on LinkedIn
@biancamillerofficial (Instagram and TikTok) – Bianca Miller-Cole on LinkedIn

Finance can be an emotional rollercoaster, so buckle up and let's ride this out together. Remember, riches come in many forms – rich in health, rich in knowledge, rich in loved ones, rich financially.

The journey of legacy doesn't stop until we are rich forever.

CHAPTER ONE
Why Money Matters

As once stated by renowned rapper and entrepreneur Shawn Carter (aka Jay-Z) 'Financial freedom is my only hope, f*ck living rich and dying broke' ('The Story of O.J.'). People are often heard quoting 'Its only money', 'money doesn't matter', 'money doesn't buy you happiness'. I hear variations on this theme expressed all the time and maybe that's not surprising. We live in a culture in which – some people at least – are quick to distance themselves from the idea that money plays an important part in their lives. The logic goes something like this: money is ever-present – no one denies that – but it's not something that should dominate your thinking; there are other more important things to focus on.

But here's what Byron and I believe. Money does matter, not necessarily for what it *is* – coins, banknotes or numbers on a bank statement – but for what it *gives* us. Whether your priority is family, travel, making music, living in a country cottage, owning a sports car, devoting your life to charitable giving, or a combination of all of the above, you will need money in order to fulfil your ambitions. It is, purely and simply, a fact of life. More than that, it's central to just about everything we choose to do. Saying money doesn't matter is a bit like saying water isn't really important.

Or to put it another way: no one wants money for its own sake. We want money because it enables us to live rich and satisfying lives. It is there to support our happiness. Money is something to celebrate.

Of course, it doesn't always work out like that. This book is being written at a time when prices are rising in the shops, energy costs are skyrocketing, central bank interest rates are on the increase around the world, and some banks are failing. Many people are struggling to buy essentials and repay debts. In this context, money can seem less like an enabler and more like a ball and chain.

That's why phrases such as 'Money doesn't matter' can be so damaging. Yes, the underlying sentiment may be sound. Money is a means to an end, not a purpose in itself. But unless you understand how money works in your own life and in the wider economy, it is easy to find that your personal finances are slipping out of control. Your money is not being used to its maximum potential.

And today, it's not just those who have always struggled to make ends meet who are feeling the pain. In today's climate, many people who have previously considered themselves to be financially comfortable may be finding it difficult to cope with rising prices and a wider sense of economic uncertainty.

Circumstances change. Rampant inflation can reduce the value of your salary If you're a homeowner, and a sudden rise in interest rates can reduce your disposable income within days or weeks of a central bank's announcement. Even if you save, the money you keep in the bank can lose value, simply because the returns don't keep pace with inflation. Investments in shares can go south. You can lose your job and find yourself with no means of support. And without some kind of financial cushion, unemployment can be disastrous.

Against this background, all of us need to be resilient. So, it isn't wrong or shallow to spend a certain amount of time thinking about your finances and how you can perhaps earn a higher income, save more, or invest in a way that provides the best possible returns.

In fact, there has never been a better time to take control and improve your financial situation.

This does not amount to an unhealthy obsession with money to the exclusion of all else. Quite the opposite. By making the most of the money you earn, you free yourself to live the life you aspire to – whatever that may be. And it's important to remember that anyone – regardless of income – can improve their financial circumstances.

On the money – a personal journey

An interest in money isn't something that is dry or impersonal. It can be a way of unlocking opportunities and understanding the world. As Byron likes to put it: 'Money really does make the world go round. My interest in money led me to a lifelong quest. I've always wanted to understand money. How does it work and what can it do for me and my loved ones? That's been something I've been exploring from my earliest days of working in a mobile phone shop and starting businesses. That ambition to understand money has been a hugely important part of my life. That understanding starts with the fundamentals: what is money?'

What is this thing called money?

But first, let's take a look at the basics. It's worth remembering that money was invented to improve how societies function while also making it easier for individuals to trade with each other. That's one of the reasons it's so important in our lives.

Until about 5,000 years ago, the only form of currency was barter. If you wanted to buy, say, clothing, you would offer something in return – a number of animals, perhaps, or pottery.

There was quite a big problem with this. Let's assume for a moment that you have a field full of sheep but you need clothes for your family because the winter is approaching. That clothing can be bought locally from a trader but unfortunately the supplier in question already has far too many sheep. More than he knows what to do with. In fact, you have nothing to offer that the trader wants. As a result, you might have to look elsewhere. At the very least, the trader might give you less than you expected for the sheep you're offering.

Money was created to address that situation. Coins and other forms of currency changed the game entirely. The coins you earned from selling your produce could be used to buy from others. There was no need to match demand and supply. You might have to negotiate on a price, but the trader who might have rejected the goods you sought to barter would be more than happy to accept your coins. It was the beginning of a recognizable economic model. The modern world had begun.

The invention of a kind of currency is usually credited to the Mesopotamians, inventors of the shekel. Initially, shekels were not coins but units of weight that could be used in transactions. We had to wait for another 4,000 years or so before the first metal coins began to appear, first in China around 1,000 BCE and then 300 years later in the Near East, where the introduction of coinage is usually attributed to King Croesus of Lydia (died 546 BCE). Currency could also be found in Egypt and what is now Turkey in around the same period.

The early experiments with money still echo in the human imagination. Even today, shekel is – in addition to being Israel's currency – a slang term for cash, and the expression 'as rich as Croesus' – aka 'filthy rich' – is still in circulation.

Then came paper money, and once again China was ahead of the game. It was introduced there in about 700 BCE. For its part, Europe didn't enjoy the privilege of using lightweight paper notes until the 17th century, with Sweden taking the lead. In the UK and USA, the first banknotes were issued in 1833 and 1861, respectively.

The banking system

Each tentative step in the development of money had a profound impact on human society. The arrival of metal coins allowed the rulers of the ancient world to pay their armies, and employers could reward workers.

Trade also became a lot easier. If, for example, a merchant wanted to travel to buy goods, it was no longer strictly necessary to take along items of a commensurate value to offer in return. For their part, sellers could store and save their coins. They could become very rich if they had goods that others wanted to buy and were skilled at negotiation. Wealth could be measured in coins and not just in land or cattle. All of this drove civilization forward. Money paid not just for big houses and palaces, but also art, music and land in cities.

The widespread adoption of paper money made it easier to trade over long distances because it was lightweight.

Money also fuelled the development of banking, which dates back to the Romans but became big business in Europe and North America during the 19th century. As individuals got richer, they needed safe places to store their coins and banknotes. Banks not only provided a secure repository, but also built services on top of their core function. With large sums stored in their vaults, they could use some of their deposits to lend to borrowers. Assuming, depositors didn't all seek to withdraw their money at the same time, this was a safe way for banks to generate revenue through interest payments. The key to the expansion of lending was a system known as fractional reserve banking. Put simply, banks were required to keep a proportion of their deposits available as liquid (available) assets. The rest could be allocated as loans. A variation on the same system underpins the banking sector today.

Fast-forward to the present where money plays a role that the pioneers of China or Mesopotamia could not have dreamed of. The modern world of money began in 1871 when Western Union began to use the US telegraph to move cash around. In this way, money became an abstract thing, detached from coins and notes. Today, banks simply use digital networks to debit or credit accounts with no redress to physical money.

Consequently, notes and coins have largely been replaced by electronic money and digital transfers. We don't quite live in a cashless society − not yet − but the day when physical currency becomes obsolete may not be far off.

Very few of us are paid in hard cash. The money we use has no physical existence until such time as a cardholder goes to a cashpoint. Increasingly, however, even small transactions are carried out using debit or credit cards or mobile payment systems such as Apple Pay.

You buy a beer and it's charged either as a debit on your account or as a debt. In addition, store cards and point-of-sale lending systems such as Klarna also provide access to credit lines, providing new ways to spend.

The new connected world of money means that most of us have access to instant credit (either through credit cards or agreed overdrafts). This is hugely convenient while exposing us to significant risk if we don't use the bank's services wisely.

All this is possible because money is an incredibly flexible concept. Whether you're talking about copper coins, notes or ones and zeros in a computerized banking system, money does not have any intrinsic value. Instead, a value is assigned to the dollar, pound, euro or yen in your pocket or bank account, and there is a social consensus (nationally and internationally) around what each unit of currency will buy regardless of the format.

Why money has value

But what gives money its value? In barter economies, any item traded – a pot, a necklace, an animal – has a physical utility and is, therefore, worth something. The same is not true of, say, a banknote. It is simply a piece of paper, or latterly some kind of polymer. So why can you go into a Starbucks and buy something tangible with it?

In the case of early coins made of gold and silver, there was, in fact, some kind of intrinsic value. People valued precious metals and that meant the coins themselves were worth something.

Fast-forward two millennia to the years after World War II and you could see an echo of this in the way some countries propped up their currencies. For instance, in the USA, the value of the dollar was underpinned (or fixed) by an agreed amount of gold. So, in theory at least, if you handed $35 to the US Government, the Treasury would be obliged to give you an ounce of gold in return. This was essentially an agreement between governments, rather than individuals. It was the way nation states and their central banks established the value of their own currencies in relation to others.

Today, the value of a given currency is fixed by something less tangible. At its simplest, the money in your pocket or bank account is worth something because the government tells us it is and we all agree. When you buy your double-shot latte from Starbucks, both purchaser and seller accept that the three or four pounds or dollars crossing the counter are equivalent to the cup of coffee that moves in the other direction.

It's not just about consensus, however. The value of money is maintained by controlling the amount of it that is circulating at any one time.

Cryptocurrencies

Cryptocurrencies illustrate the relationship between the value of money and the amount available. Put simply, cryptocurrencies are newly created digital currencies that exist independently of governments, central banks and the established financial system.

The best known of these is bitcoin, an electronic, virtual coin that was essentially created out of thin air by Satoshi Nakamoto (a pseudonym). There are many others. According to the 'cryptocurrency comparison website' BitStacker, there were more than 20,000 individual currencies in existence at the close of 2022.

On the face of it, cryptocurrencies perform much the same kind of function as conventional money. You can buy and pay for things with cryptocurrencies and, because the value of individual coins goes up and down, you can also invest in them.

Unlike the money that gets transferred from bank to bank when you make a purchase on your debit card, cryptocurrencies are not underpinned by government policy and nor do they depend on the traditional financial infrastructure. A bitcoin transaction doesn't go through a bank or payment system. Instead, all transactions are logged on vast and decentralized electronic ledgers spread across multiple computer networks using a technology known as blockchain.

The key to the value of cryptocurrencies is supply and demand. Supply is limited by the creators, and as demand rises the value of each coin (unit of currency) rises. And, like traditional currencies, forces in the market can push the value of certain cryptocurrencies to stratospheric heights. Equally, the currency can crash, leaving those holding it ruined or, at the very least, nursing a very painful financial hangover. However, consensus also plays a part. Cryptocurrencies have a value because there are enough people in the world who are willing to buy into the concept.

We will focus on cryptocurrencies later, in Chapter 9, and share how we really feel about crypto!

Even a very quick recap of the line of history that runs from barter to bitcoin illustrates that money can take many forms. Equally, it provides us with an ever-increasing array of opportunities. The money we earn can be put in a bank where it will earn interest. It can be spent on consumer goods, holidays or long-term assets such as property. Equally, it can be actively invested in shares, bonds, art, antiques or wine. When these assets can rise in value, they can be sold at a profit. Your wealth can grow depending on how you spend or invest. If you're lucky, it can provide you with an income that doesn't require any additional work on your part.

The problem with money

So, yes, money makes life easier, but not always. We live within a hugely complex financial system, and there are times when the forces that move the value of currencies seem out of control.

The value of our money can rise and fall, even when it's doing nothing more exciting than sitting in a bank.

That much became painfully obvious in the wake of the COVID-19 pandemic and the escalation of the Russian invasion of Ukraine beginning in 2022 when the world's economy seemed to go into a tailspin. Oil and gas prices rose, pushing up inflation to levels of 10, 15 or even 20 per cent, depending on where you happened to live.

Higher inflation meant that the pound, euro and dollar bought fewer items, so essentially money became less valuable very quickly. If you had £10,000 deposited in a bank account, it was still ostensibly £10,000. But in terms of the goods or services that money could buy, it was perhaps worth only £9,000. According to Sky News, the cost of milk, cheese and eggs – things perceived to be basics – have risen at the fastest pace in 45 years. For example, in the UK supermarket Morrisons the cost of a block of Cheddar cheese increased by 50 per cent from £1.50 in December 2022 to £2.25 in February 2023.

This is something that affects everyone, particularly the less well off. The depreciation of money is something that everyone should be aware of.

Meanwhile, the world – or a very large part of it – entered a period of very low growth, with some countries seeing their economies slip into recession. There were multiple reasons. In the aftermath of COVID, the 'supply chains' that carry raw materials, components and products around the world weren't running at full capacity. This affected businesses, which couldn't always buy the things they needed in order to trade. Inflation began to rise because shortages pushed up prices. This process was exacerbated by the war in Ukraine. Oil, gas and food prices soared as supplies faltered.

Wages struggled to keep up with prices and that was a double whammy. Just as money in the bank was worth less so were monthly salaries. Doubtless, a great many people came to the conclusion that the financial system was somehow broken – that all the certainties were slipping away.

Taking control and cutting through the jargon

It's easy to feel that way, not least because discussions about the world of money are couched in so much mysterious jargon. Central banks raise their 'base rates' to control inflation. Why do they do that? They also engage in the obscure practice known as quantitative easing.

And that's when we begin to drown in the jargon. Bryon and I both studied economics at university, so we were pretty much on top of the vocabulary of money. But 'quantitative easing' – that was something we hated studying.

And yet we all hear on the news that quantitative easing is used to stimulate growth. How does that work exactly? And why do falling bond prices put pressure on mortgages. Why are we paying more to borrow while prices rise in the shops? Joining up dots is difficult, especially for those with no grounding in the way money works.

And yet, in order to manage your own finances, you need to understand a bit about the wider economy and how it functions.

When inflation becomes a problem

Let's start with inflation. As I write, it's 2023, and the last time I checked, inflation was running above 10 per cent in the UK. With a bit of variation, it's a similar story across Europe and North America.

When we use the term 'inflation', we are really talking about what consumers pay for the things they buy. Inflation is measured by tracking prices within a 'basket' of goods and services. The imaginary basket will contain common food items, electronic goods, clothes, energy and a host of other things. Price increases (or falls) are measured against a year earlier and averaged out. That average is known as the inflation rate.

A certain amount of inflation is generally not considered a bad thing. Quite the opposite. Economists will tell you that, in normal times, an inflation rate of 2.00–2.5 per cent is, generally speaking, beneficial. For one thing, moderate price rises are an indicator that the economy is performing well. If inflation is too low, say at zero or in negative territory, it usually means the economy is experiencing problems. Static or falling prices point to low demand for goods or services. That makes it hard for companies to sustain existing prices and pay their employees.

Moderate inflation, on the other hand, is helpful to those of us who are making payments on mortgages or long-term debts. Let's say you buy a house with a mortgage of £2,000 a month. If inflation is running at 2.5 per cent a year, the chances are that salaries will also rise by that amount or more. Thus in ten years' time – assuming the monthly repayments are similar – the mortgage will siphon off a smaller proportion of your salary, giving you a higher level of disposable income.

It's also argued that inflation running at about 2.0 per cent stimulates consumption. Consumers buy now because the cost will be more expensive in the future. This is helpful to businesses.

All that flips on its head when inflation rises to 5, 10, 12 or 20 per cent and becomes unpredictable. Over the longer term, rising inflation will result in an even bigger reduction of debt in proportion to income. But in the short or medium term, if wages don't keep up, rapidly rising prices reduce the unit value of money and many people will struggle to buy groceries, pay bills and heat their homes. They might not get a chance to see their mortgage debt eaten away over ten years, if it's impossible to make the payments in the here and now.

Added to that is the fact that central banks tend to respond to inflation by pushing up interest rates, often very rapidly. Mortgages become more expensive to pay off, as do credit card bills and other forms of debt. Assuming inflation subsides, this is a short-term problem but it is no less real for that.

All these factors illustrate why, at time of writing, many people are struggling. There are just too many pressures on household budgets.

So what makes inflation happen?

Inflation is triggered by a number of factors often working in tandem with each other. Supply and demand play a big role. If demand for products within an economy outstrips the ability of the same economy to deliver goods and services, prices rise.

Demand can be fuelled by the amount of money in circulation. For instance, if credit is widely available and cheap, that increases the ability of consumers to buy goods. Effectively there is more money around, albeit borrowed. The result can be a consumer boom. This, in turn, fuels consumer price inflation as retailers push up prices to take advantage of the spending bonanza.

But prices also rise because business costs go up. For instance, massive increases in oil and gas prices due to the war in Ukraine have not only increased the cost of petrol and home heating but also made it more expensive for businesses to operate. If you run a restaurant or a bakery – or indeed any energy-hungry company – a big jump in electricity or gas prices can mean the difference between being profitable and going bust. This in turn means we pay more to go to restaurants or buy bread.

And naturally enough, when living costs spiral upward, employees tend to ask for higher wage settlements to maintain living standards. Again, this creates inflationary pressure, unless the improved pay is matched by higher productivity. A lack of balance between supply and demand in the labour market is also a factor. If there are not enough workers to fill available vacancies, it becomes a seller's market for job candidates. They ask for – and often get – higher salaries. In the post-pandemic period, many workers quit their jobs to take early retirement, a trend dubbed the 'Great Resignation'. Employers struggled to find skilled staff and had to pay more to bring them on board.

What central banks really fear is an inflation psychology. Once people become accustomed to high inflation and expect it to continue, they make financial decisions accordingly – for instance, asking for big pay increases. This embeds inflation into a semi-permanent national mindset, making it more difficult to rein in.

Why interest rates rise

That raises another question. At times when many people are struggling because of high prices, why do central banks make things even worse by raising borrowing rates? Doesn't this mean even more people, particularly homeowners, will struggle?

Typically, central banks set inflation targets of 2.0 to 2.5 per cent. If consumer price pressures rise, the likelihood is that the bank will raise interest rates. This is intended to suppress demand. The logic is that consumers have less money, so they spend less. Similarly, employers borrow less for investment. Again, there is less money flowing. With fewer goods being bought, the laws of supply and demand kick in. Prices fall.

So on the face of it is a fairly simple equation. When inflationary pressures start to build, central banks ease on the brakes by raising interest rates. At other times, when the economy is weak, a bank might lower rates to stimulate demand.

The key tool is the base rate. Central banks like the Federal Reserve System in the USA and the Bank of England in the UK actually do quite a lot of lending to commercial banks in order to keep the economy flowing. The base rate designates the interest charged on loans to commercial banks that are repaid rapidly. When the base rate rises, commercial banks pass this on to borrowers. Consequently, mortgage, loan and credit card costs rise. Savers may get more in interest rates, but that's not guaranteed.

In an ideal world, everything would be in balance. The free market economist Friedrich Hayek (1899–1992) argued there was an optimal level for interest rates in any economy. When set too high they reduce demand and dampen growth. If set too low, they offer little incentive for saving and also push demand to unsustainable levels. Such imbalances, he argued, are the cause of the so-called boom-and-bust economic cycles that we've seen in the past.

So the job of central banks is to find the right balance, which will always be shifting according to economic circumstances. But, in recent years, it really hasn't been that easy.

Bonds and quantitative easing

But let's return to my university days and the dreaded quantitative easing.

When the threat of a recession looms due to lower demand, the central banks do the opposite of raising rates. To boost demand, they pump money into the economy – as they did after the great financial crisis of 2007/2008. Usually, this isn't done by printing money. Instead, banks buy government and corporate bonds.

Like shares, bonds are simply investments that are bought with the expectation of receiving a return. Governments issue them (when they're known as gilts) as do companies. But although mentioned frequently on the news, they are not widely understood. And yet events in the bond market can have a direct impact on our wealth.

Bonds are essentially time-limited IOUs. Buyers lend the sellers money. This will be repaid with interest over an agreed period of time that could be five, ten or twenty years. In that respect, each bond represents a debt that has to be honoured. The issuer owes the buyer money. But bonds can also be traded, and, like shares, their prices fluctuate according to demand.

Because bonds are representative of money owed, their value depends on whether the market considers the issuing organization to be a safe or risky proposition. If the market gets worried about a particular bond issuer's ability to repay the debt, the price falls. This has the impact of pushing up the interest repayment (or yield) as a percentage of the bond's value. This is the market's way of pricing in risk.

Flip that on its head and higher bond prices reduce the yield. That's why central banks buy bonds to stimulate their countries' economies. Falling bond interest yields put downward pressure on the rates payable on more commonplace debts such as mortgages. This puts more money into the hands of consumers and businesses, in the hope of delivering an economic boost.

Why the economy looks broken

But here's why things went awry in the wake of the pandemic. Inflation was rising not because of consumer demand in Western economies but because oil and gas prices were pushing up costs for just about everyone and supply chains were broken.

Rather than a demand-led boom scenario – one that could be controlled by higher interest rates – central bankers were looking at that rarest of things – inflation coupled not with a buoyant economy but with either recession or years of zero or very low growth.

This created a huge dilemma for central banks – one that was particularly acute in the UK. As inflation began to take hold, the Bank of England raised interest rates slowly. Some said too slowly. Others said raising rates would trigger a recession, and there were even arguments in favour of more quantitative easing to stimulate demand.

The crunch point came when the government announced a plan for growth that would involve billions of pounds in new borrowing to fund tax cuts. The markets thought the policy was reckless and sold UK government bonds, pushing up yields. This rapidly fed through to higher borrowing rates on loans and mortgages.

Taxing and spending

All of this illustrates the close relationship between *monetary* policy – which is usually discharged by central banks – and *fiscal* policy. The latter is essentially related to tax and spending and is carried out by governments.

In order to spend, governments must either tax or borrow. If they choose to borrow, lenders (who buy government bonds) will assess the risk. The higher the perceived risk, the greater the expected return on government bonds will be. As we've seen, the interest rates in government bonds go a long way to dictate what the rest of us will pay when we borrow money. Low confidence in a government ultimately feeds through to higher mortgage rates, even if that seems unfair.

Currency prices

There is one more factor influencing the value of the money in your pocket – namely, the international value of the currency you use.

Currencies don't exist in isolation. They bump up against each other. So-called fiat currencies, such as the euro, sterling and dollar, aren't pegged to assets and they float free on international markets. Healthy economies tend to have strong currencies, but when market traders sense weakness – or when they think domestic interest rates are too low – they will sell one currency and buy another. When a currency is sold, it weakens against its peers.

We tend to notice this most acutely when we go on holiday. When the pound was worth almost two dollars, back in the 1990s, Britons found their money went a long way when they visited the USA. Today, the pound is weak against the dollar, making transatlantic trips much more expensive.

There is a domestic effect, too. If your home currency is weak, imported goods, such as consumer electronics, will be more expensive. In other words, a weak currency is inflationary.

Given what has been happening over the past few years, you might look at the world and wonder if the economic problems we all face are in danger of becoming overwhelming. And from the point of view of your personal finances, you might question whether making plans and thinking about the medium and long term is even worth it. No one could deny that a lot of people are feeling poorer and the future seems unpredictable. And why save when the value of your money could be simply wiped out?

I'm here to tell you that taking a proactive approach to finance is more vital than ever. There are many people who face real hardship because of higher food, energy and housing costs. It can seem overwhelming.

But whatever your situation, managing money well can help you ride out short-term problems. Saving helps you deal more easily. Investing – whether in a pension or assets such as shares – builds up resilience for the long term. It's all about planning and good practices.

Understanding your options

As you make plans, it's important to be aware of the big picture, but to really take control, it's equally important to understand your own personal finance options. If you're reading this book, the chances are that you are looking for ways and means to manage your financial affairs more effectively and (hopefully) make your money work harder.

Being wealthy, rich or simply comfortable means different things to different people, but the same principles of savings and investment can be applied regardless of your circumstances and ambitions. You just need to know what's open to you.

There are plenty of savings and investment opportunities. If you open a Sunday newspaper and turn to the personal finance pages, you will find information on savings accounts, unit trusts, share trading, buy-to-let investment and a whole host of other tempting investment opportunities. You will probably also find articles about how to manage debt or find the best mortgage offer.

The problem is, perhaps, the world of personal finance is also packed with jargon and that can be a deterrent.

Writers will talk about APR, AER, income, equity investment, shares, bonds, cryptocurrencies, yields and unit trusts without providing any real explanation. It's assumed that everyone is steeped in the lore and vocabulary of the financial services industry.

Actually, the jargon is not that complicated once you get to grips with it, and one of the purposes of this book is to demystify money while putting you on the right track to optimize your own financial affairs.

There are a few terms that you should get to grips with very quickly, especially at a time of volatile interest rates. **APR** (annualized percentage rate) is one of them. It seems straightforward enough. For instance, if the APR on a loan is 5 per cent, then that's the amount of interest you pay over a year. However, if a loan is paid off over a five-year period, you'll pay more than 5 per cent because the annualized interest is calculated over a longer period. So what you really need to know is what the total cost of the loan will be over five years and how much the monthly repayment will be.

Conversely, on a credit card, a 20 per cent APR will be incredibly cheap if the debt is repaid over a month or two after you buy an item but monstrously expensive if you let it run for a year or more.

Understanding what the APR actually means allows you to make sensible borrowing decisions.

For savers, it's also worth calculating what your **AER** (annualized equivalent rate) savings rate delivers over a period of time. Savings accounts offer interest on the money you've deposited but perhaps also bonuses. An AER tells you the total that you will earn over a year, including bonuses and charges. Both APR and AER are directly linked to events in the wider economy.

But let's look beyond savings to investment. None of the terms you'll hear are overly complicated. Shares are essentially units of ownership in a company. You can purchase shares in private companies or more commonly in businesses that are listed on a stock exchange. Their shares can be easily bought and sold. When you buy shares, you have equity in the company. That is simply the value of the investment. We've spoken about bonds already. When you buy a bond from an issuer, you are lending money and will be repaid with interest after a set term.

You'll also hear people talking about **assets**. No mysteries here, either. In investment terms, an asset is something you own in order to get a financial benefit. Your assets could be shares, bonds or property. Income is the money you receive from an asset. Income can be regular (paid monthly or annually) or be realized when the asset is sold. Investment assets can deliver income, growth or both. Income is money generated by the asset and paid to the holder on a regular basis. For instance, annual dividends from a share portfolio is income. Growth comes from the appreciation of the asset. For example, you buy a property for £300,000 and in a year's time it is worth £400,000. Growth is all about rising value. You buy a share, its value grows, and you make a profit when you sell it. Some assets are better for income – you get regular payments. Some are more suitable as longer-term growth prospects.

Some assets do both very well. Byron and I are both keen on property for this simple reason: a rental property provides monthly income, but if house prices are rising, there should be a significant profit if and when the property is sold.

Your return on an investment is simply the profit you make, rendered as a percentage rate.

The bigger point here is that money really does matter, and in difficult economic times financial literacy is becoming increasingly important. It's not just about the vocabulary; it's about knowing how the world of money operates and making it work for you.

Throughout the rest of this book, we will use our experience to demystify the world of money for you.

The Rich Forever checklist

- Acknowledge the importance of money in your life. Regardless of your personal and professional ambitions and goals, sound money management will make it easier to do the things you want to do.
- The world of finance can seem mystifying but take time to understand the forces that affect the value of the money you've worked hard for.
- Times are tough, but everyone can manage their finances better by beginning to save, invest and clear debts.
- Understand the jargon of the finance industry and what it means in terms of your savings, investment and borrowing options.
- Use this knowledge to underpin your own financial planning.

CHAPTER TWO
Developing Your Money Mindset

As someone smart once said, 'It's not how much money you have. It's how much you keep.' We have all had experiences that have shaped who we are today. The way we were brought up not only affects us as children but shapes the way we see the world and respond to it – perhaps for our entire lives. The same can be said of our experiences with friends, partners and co-workers. They all have an impact on who we are and how we see things.

And just as we have a history with people, we also have a history with money. Your attitude to the money you earn and how you save it or invest is shaped by lessons good and bad that you've learned in the past.

And when you begin to join up the dots you can see that your history with money is probably heavily influenced by the people who have meant the most to you. Family, friends, partners and peers all play their part in setting examples and giving you advice. Often your parents and close family exert the biggest influence – although how that plays out can be complicated.

So how does your relationship with money start?

This is something I often talk about with Bianca. She grew up in a family where she could see how hard her parents worked and that was a good lesson. But there were good times and bad. Or, to put it another way, there were periods when there seemed to be plenty of money around but that wasn't always the case. There were certainly times when the family finances were tight.

'To be honest, there were occasions when I thought my parents weren't as focused on saving money as I thought they should have been. Indeed, my dad was very good at making money and spending money. He enjoyed his expensive suits and Gucci shoes,' she says. 'I could also see some generational differences. My grandfather was a really big saver and so was my grandmother.'

Looking back, Bianca feels family experience helped her to understand the value of money and also appreciate the things that it can buy. 'My parents sent me to private school because they were determined that I should get a good education. For my 21st birthday they bought me an inscribed Rolex watch. I knew neither of those things came easy and shouldn't be taken for granted.'

Bianca will often tell you that she is cautious with money. 'Considered' might be a better word. Until the age of 21 she was focused on saving and tended to avoid spending too much on things like shoes and handbags. But by 17 she had her own car, by 22 she was on the property ladder, and by 24 she had invested those early savings in her own business.

So, although she can be cautious and likes to save, she is also a believer in flipping things around – for instance, switching from saving to borrowing mode when that's the right thing to do. In the early days of her business, when it wasn't generating much income, she was happy to use her credit card to live on until things picked up.

It is this positive relationship with money that Bianca has been able to share by providing advice to family and friends.

The bigger point here is that managing money well is not always about saving or even investing. Sometimes to achieve your goals, you may need to borrow, either on a credit card, a bank loan or a mortgage. That may be to keep going while your business grows or to buy the home which will give a degree of financial strength. The thing to remember is that, at any given time, your approach to managing money should be enabling you rather than holding you back.

Of course, everyone's relationship with money is different. And everyone defines that relationship differently.

Personally, I'm always finding ways to make money work harder. I'm always looking for ways to make more.

Now, I'm very far from reckless. Actually, I have a medium tolerance for risk, but I'm always thinking, 'What's the worst that can happen?' And having assessed the risk, I'm prepared to invest in anything and everything if the opportunity looks good.

That's partly because I don't really fear the worst. My experience tells me that one setback won't result in a crisis because I know the money will flow. Why? Because I have multiple skills and a great network.

So Bianca and I are different, but complementary. We're mutually supportive and prepared to help each other out. That's important. When it comes to partners, as Bianca's grandmother would say, 'It's always good to have a helpmate rather than help-weight'.

What is your relationship with money?

Everyone has a relationship with money but we don't always think in those terms. Sometimes it helps to break things down and get things in perspective. How do you do that? Well, try taking a minute to answer these few simple questions.

- How would you define your relationship with money as it stands today?
- Are you in debt or would you consider yourself comfortably off?
- Are you saving – perhaps for a pension – or spending every penny you have as soon as it hits your bank account?
- Are you thinking about investing? Is it something you're doing or considering. Or does it seem like something that really isn't for you?
- Why are you doing or not doing these things? What are your drivers?
- What do your answers say about your relationship with money?

The money mindset

At least some aspects of your approach to money are likely to be learned from or influenced by other people. Unless you begin to unpack what that means, this learned behaviour may not be serving you well.

If there was one single money mindset, we would all be doing much the same thing. That would probably involve managing our income and outgoings well to ensure we have cash in the bank. We would save for safety and invest in shares, bonds or other assets for higher returns. We would use debt sensibly (I'll go into that in more detail later) and not max out on our credit cards without a clear goal and a means of repaying the debt as quickly as possible. And we would feel confident enough to invest in ourselves. I could go on.

But there isn't a single approach to money. Life isn't like that.

So what are the factors in your past that shape your financial situation today?

- Was money abundant in your home and what did that teach you? Or was it scarce?
- Was there a need to scratch around for cash just to fund the basics of living?
- And what did you learn from your parents and other family members?

Crucially, how did you respond to what was going on around you? There isn't necessarily a straight line that can be drawn between a certain scenario – say frequent hard times as a child – and your attitude to money now. It's a question of interpretation. You may have formed a fatalistic view that 'hard times' was your lot in life. Something that was already written into the story of how your life would unfold.

But I have to say that being fatalistic doesn't really get you anywhere. Even without the current wonders that social media has now provided to the current generation, I still knew that my current circumstances of growing up on a poverty-stricken council estate would not incarcerate my mind. That might have been my present but it definitely would not be my future.

A poverty mindset

The danger here is that you slip into what is known as a poverty mindset. You struggle to make ends meet, living from one salary slip to the next. Bills and debts pile up. Now there are a great many people who find themselves in that situation, either temporarily or over the long term. But a poverty mindset cements the situation. There is always a voice in your head telling you that things really won't get better.

This kind of mindset is something that should be unlearned as quickly as possible.

But the poverty mindset is not an inevitable response to hard times, either as a child or later in life. You can learn positive lessons from what you saw going on around you and use them to keep your financial story on track. Clearly, the second approach is the best one, but it's not always easy to understand how the experiences so far in your life have shaped you. It requires reflection.

A fear of money

Even if you feel comfortable financially, there are psychological traps that you can slip into – obstacles that can prevent you from using the cash you earn as effectively as possible.

Fear of money is one of them. Let me give you an example. Let's say you work hard, save and build a pretty good life. The bills are paid on time, you don't have any concerns about meeting the rent or the mortgage payment, and there's enough left over to do the things you like to do. Everything is looking good.

But it could be that because of lessons learned in the past, you are always worried about slipping into debt or being unable to pay a bill. Perhaps you are overly cautious when spending and don't enjoy life quite as much as you should.

Some people are uncomfortable with the prospect of having too much money. They feel that somehow it wouldn't be good for them to focus on earning more or investing more. It's a feeling that can go back to childhood. If you were raised in a family where money wasn't discussed or prioritized and where ambition wasn't really part of the familial DNA, you may feel that success will somehow separate you from your family and friends.

Alternatively, you could be afraid to take a calculated risk. Perhaps you have a great business idea but are reluctant to find the funds to get it off the ground. Or you back away from doing a degree because of the financial outlay involved. This is a different kind of caution, and it can also be learned from childhood. A voice in your head tells you that playing safe is the best option. Taking a risk could bring everything down around your ears. You don't invest in yourself.

Fear of communication

In addition to a fear of money itself, there can also be a reluctance – sometimes stretching to a terror – of actually talking about it. You see this in a whole range of settings. In marriages, there can be a reluctance to discuss the family finances, even to the extent that real problems are ignored or covered up. For instance, household debts might rise to unsustainable levels, simply because one or both parties find it impossible to discuss budgets without getting into a row. Individuals can also be secretive about their own finances, particularly when problems are arising.

It has to be said that even outside families money can be a tricky issue to raise – at dinner parties for example – even at times like the present, when we are all living through a financial crisis. It has probably never been a more relevant time to share financial problems or, indeed, advice.

So let's begin to bring this out into the open.

Where are you now? – a checklist

If all this seems just a little bit abstract, take a look at where you are now.

Again, you can break this down into a few questions to ask yourself:

- How are things going with your life, financially and generally?
- What is your financial situation? Are you in debt or finance positive?
- How much do you earn?
- Do you live from pay check to pay check?
- Can you make ends meet or do you find yourself borrowing to stay alive.

And there is a bigger, overarching question: How do you feel about your financial situation? Are you where you want to be?

The truth is that taking a long hard look at your financial history tends to throw your present circumstances into sharp relief. At the very least, it can help you identify some of the behaviours you've developed. And where necessary you can improve things.

Who are you?

But there's another question and a fundamental one. When it comes to money, who are you exactly? Are you someone who likes to save for a rainy day? Or do you prefer to invest? Or perhaps you do both.

You could express this in slightly different terms. The concept of the rainy day is closely tied to the need we all have for a safety net when things go wrong. So, if you lose your job or your business goes bust, there is cash in the bank to see you through. A bank savings account does represent an investment – albeit one that offers a low rate of return – but it's not your only option. Higher returns are available, but usually the risk of losing money is also greater.

Even in something relatively safe like a unit trust (a vehicle for investing collectively with others in a managed portfolio of shares), the value of your investment can go up as well as down. And there are other factors to consider. In some investments your cash will be tied up for specified periods of time. You might have a lot of wealth tied up in investments but be short of cash.

So who are you, what are you looking for and what is your tolerance for risk? These are the broad questions that you should ask yourself.

You could, of course, be someone who spends money as quickly as it comes in, owning a lot of short-term and rapidly depreciating assets, such as cars and clothes but having nothing left in your financial tank at the end of the month.

If that is the case, I would encourage you ask yourself: who do you want to be?

If you're reading this book, I'm assuming that your sights have been set on improving your financial position in the longer term, so let's look at some goals.

Financial freedom

One thing I'm confident you *don't* want to be – consciously at least – is someone who leads a constrained life because money has become a trap. The constraints could be caused by debt or because there isn't enough money coming in to support your life and the aspirations you have. Maybe it's hard to make ends meet. For whatever reason, you don't feel free.

Let's pause for a second and think about the term 'financial freedom'. You hear it a lot nowadays. It's discussed by financial gurus on YouTube. It's written about in newspapers and (perhaps more comprehensively) in the specialist investment press. You could go so far as to say there is a financial freedom movement.

What exactly is financial freedom?

Financial freedom is something many people aspire to, but what is it? It can mean different things to different people, but there is a broadly accepted definition: financial freedom is having enough money to pay your bills and live the life you want to live without having to work day-to-day or commit any time at all to generating money.

This definition tends to be used by those who are doing well enough in life to see a future beyond the nine-to-five job. There are various ways to achieve that kind of freedom. You start a business, grow it and sell it for a life-changing sum of money. Or you take the same business to a level where you can step back, appoint other people to run it, and live off the share dividends. Or you make high-return investments in, say, start-up companies. Perhaps financial freedom is achieved later in life when the time comes to cash in your occupational pension.

Away from the dictionary definition, you might see freedom through a different lens. You want simply to be able to pay the bills without having to worry. That is a fundamental kind of freedom. It's the freedom from fear that someday there won't be enough money to cover the gas, power and telecoms costs or have holidays and support your children or parents if they need help. It's really freedom from want and is a perfectly admirable aim.

Between these two poles, there's a spectrum. Financial freedom in the short term may be about getting by with no debt. Or the goal could be to earn more and use that money to become wealthier through saving and investment, making life easier in the process. At the end of the spectrum you are at the point when income is divorced from the need to work. Your money is working so hard that you don't have to.

So which of these is right for you? It's important to define your own terms and adopt the financial strategies that will allow you to measure your success. And we can all move along the spectrum. We can journey towards ever greater financial freedom. As we progress through life, our sights can be raised higher.

Knowing your number

A good first step is to define what your financial ambitions are. You can think of this as 'knowing your number'.

Looking at the short, medium and long term, what do you want your life to look like and what do you need to earn to achieve, maintain and sustain that desired lifestyle? In answering this, try not to be vague. It's best if you can put some hard figures on it. Remember also, the income you command doesn't sit in isolation. Its value is, to a very great extent, dictated by your outgoings – for instance, what you are spending (or planning to spend) on a mortgage or rent and the sums you expect to save or invest.

To come up with a number you really have to do a full audit of your current financial position and what you expect it to look like in the future. It's best to do that in a structured way. To that end we have provided an online resource that will help you audit your finances. You can find it at: www.selfmadebook.uk

Deciding on a number can be a useful psychological tool. By pinning down the figure you want to hit, you set a marker for yourself. You have a target to aim for and you'll know if you miss it. It's motivation.

Targeting a number also provides a means to keep things real. It's actually not that difficult to acquire material things. If you have a credit card with a high spending limit, very little is out of bounds. You might struggle to buy a new car with a platinum card, but you can certainly go down to the shops and buy expensive clothes and accessories. Or if travel is your thing, tickets to exotic destinations are there at your fingertips when you open a laptop or open an app on your phone.

So there's an important distinction to be made, between the luxuries you can afford and those that are funded on a buy–now–pay later basis. The truth is that some people look rich, but behind the facade they are in debt and struggling. Other people earn very little and are careful about their spending but manage to save.

I really want to stress that spending above your means is a fast track to poverty. Setting a number helps you know exactly what needs to be done to attain the life you aspire to.

Too much too fast – the perils of windfalls

Unless you know how to manage the money you have, there is a really high chance that you will struggle to hold on to your wealth in the medium or longer term.

Money management can be a particular problem for those who come into vast sums of money quickly or over a relatively short time-frame. Lottery winners who become rich overnight are a case in point. People with highly paid but time-limited careers, such as athletes or pop stars, can also hit difficulties.

You might assume that acquiring wealth overnight would be a good thing. After all, it's what a lot of people dream of, but that isn't always the case. There are a great many press reports suggesting that lottery winners are particularly prone to financial ruin.

We have to tread cautiously here. A few years ago, the US-based National Endowment for Financial Education (NEFE) reportedly said that around 70 per cent of lottery winners ended up bankrupt or with nothing. This was widely reported but the headline finding was slightly inaccurate. The NEFE set up a council to look at the impact of lottery wins on the recipients. The 70 per cent figure was discussed by council members based on their own experience but it didn't appear when the research was finalized.

But we do know from press reports – and this is an international phenomenon – that winning a large sum of money doesn't guarantee long-term comfort, let alone financial freedom. Many lottery winners have indeed ended up broke.

There are a number of reasons why this can happen. It can be down to simple recklessness. The lottery winners who splash out on houses, cars and a luxury lifestyle without thinking about how they will sustain their way of living over years and decades are the stuff of legend. A million pounds or dollars (admittedly at the lower end of national lottery jackpots) is a big number but it can be surprisingly easy to spend that kind of sum within months.

Of course, not everyone is reckless or feckless. Other lottery winners run into difficulties because they are too generous. When they are crowned winners and the money hits their bank accounts, they have a natural and very noble urge to help people out – friends, family, charities. Again, a very large sum of money can be spent in a short space of time. Generosity is a good thing. But it is only possible to assist people if you yourself are in a good place financially.

Then there are the consequences of poor decision making. For instance, a winner may be keen to make his or her money work as hard as possible. That's a good thing, but only if you know what you're doing or find an adviser who is both financially competent and trustworthy.

In some jurisdictions, tax is payable on winnings. Money is spent and there's nothing left when the taxman comes calling.

It would be wrong to single out lottery winners. Movie stars, athletes, musicians and sometimes even business owners can make and lose fortunes. In 2017 Moneyinc.com published a list of 20 athletes who 'went broke'. These weren't small timers. The roll call included Mike Tyson, Diego Maradona, O. J. Simpson and Evander Holyfield.

Now, there is no single story, but the common factor is an influx of wealth coupled with limited earnings potential over a lifetime.

The importance of investment

So the challenge is to make the cash work. That requires an investment strategy capable of delivering a long-term income rather than a dwindling reserve. The need to do this is very obvious in the case of athletes, celebrities and lottery winners. But the same principle applies to just about everyone. Even if you plan to go on working – and generating income – over a lifetime, it makes sense to put aside some of the money you have and invest it. That will cause your wealth to grow. You won't be solely dependent on the monthly wage packet or the profits from a business you run.

For many people, proactive investment – above and beyond regular saving – is something of an alien concept, and even for those who regularly put money into, say, shares or high-return savings schemes, we're still talking about a rainy day scenario. Investing in opportunities that might provide real income – rather than enhanced savings – is something that is seen as too risky. Something that other people do.

It's absolutely right to be cautious. It's important to adopt an approach to investment that you're comfortable with.

Questions to ask

But what does that mean in practice?

When someone tells me they want to invest I usually say something like this: 'That's absolutely great, but before you do, let's ask some questions.'

Investment checklist

- How much money do you have to invest?
- How much money do you need to invest to hit your number we spoke about earlier?
- What is your risk profile. You could boil this down to a simple question: how much are you prepared to lose?
- What are your investment goals?

Let's dig a little deeper. It's not always easy to pin down a personal risk profile, but you can think of it in terms of how much risk you are prepared to accept. Let's say you lose £5,000 on an investment. In purely financial terms that could be extremely annoying but affordable in that you wouldn't face any real hardship. Psychologically, however, you might not be prepared to take that hit. That's a negotiation you will have to have with yourself and perhaps also with a financial adviser.

Then there is the question of goals. Are you looking for 'passive income'? This is money that you don't have to work for – an investment that delivers you an income. it could be small, it could be large, but it goes into your bank account monthly or annually. Meanwhile, the original investment remains in place, earning you more money.

If you have more than one investment, then you will have more than one source of passive income. For instance, renting out a property might be one stream; a small business in which you have a share but which you don't run could be another.

Multiple passive incomes have a hedging effect. Let's say, the business you've invested in goes through a bad patch. Well, that's not great, but you're OK because of the money coming in from property rentals.

Not all investments deliver an income. Some are designed to deliver what is known as growth. You invest in an asset and make your money when it is sold. Walk through certain parts of any big city and you'll see apartments that are empty. That's not because no one wants to rent them out. They are owned by people who are using property to bank their wealth, and as property prices move upwards (as they tend to do) they will ultimately sell at a big profit. In the meantime, they stay pristine and unlived in.

You can have income and growth in the same investment. A buy-to-let property will provide a monthly income, but it can also be sold for profit at some stage in the future.

A few years ago, the US Internal Revenue Service (IRS) studied the tax returns of a selected group of millionaires. After crunching the numbers, the researchers found that, on average, millionaires have seven revenue streams – or, to be more precise, seven classes of revenue streams. Other surveys have come up with similar results.

Multiple income streams are very much part of the strategy of wealthy people. These can be passive or active (depending on whether some work is required), but working in tandem they combine to preserve and grow the income of the individual concerned.

Seven typical income streams

(*source:* IRS)

1. There will probably be **investment income** from assets such as shares. These provide not only income from dividends but also growth if the value of the shares rise.

2. Then there could be **royalty income**. We mostly tend to think of royalties in terms of cash paid to musicians or writers when copies of their work are sold (or, in the case of music, streamed). They own the rights and are entitled to a share of the profit. Over time this becomes passive income because the work needs to be done only once. The same principle applies to intellectual property. You might own the patent on a certain type of microchip. Every time it is sold, you get a royalty or licence payment.

3 The aforementioned **property income** is popular. This can be grown by buying multiple properties, all generating rental income and possibly additional sums from extras such as concierge services.

4 **Interest from savings** – this will be the investment starting point for a lot of people.

5 **Earnings from a day job.** Whether you're an employee working at a local business, or the CEO of a multinational, the work you do every day may well form the biggest component of your income. However, if you're able – as you get older – to cut back on the hours you work, other income streams will become more important.

6 **Profits from any business** that you own.

7 **Capital gains** could also play a part in your wealth creation plans – for instance, when you sell shares, property or a business you've built. This is in addition to any regular dividend or rental payments.

Is having multiple income streams just for the wealthy? The IRS was looking at the financial habits of millionaires, so is there anything that is relevant to those who are not (as yet) quite as prosperous. Multiple income streams – and you could start with two – provide you with greater financial security, even if, at first, they only pay out a small amount of money.

As your portfolio grows, you could be on your way to financial freedom. So let's start where you are now and go from there. Take out a pen and paper or fire up your computer and do the following:

- List your current income streams.
- List your planned income streams, looking at the opportunities available to you and how can you bring more money on stream.

Opportunities

In order to invest, you'll need a number of things. First and foremost, you need something to invest in. It isn't hard to find an opportunity to invest in retail investment products. For example, you can save into a unit trust. Or you can choose to own shares directly. There are plenty of online services that will help you to do that. Some are for beginners. Some will (effectively) pair you with professionals. Others are designed for pros. There are specialist services, too – for instance, share trading platforms that focus on ethical companies or green investments.

But opportunities are not always obvious or accessible. You could for example seek out property investment opportunities by going to local auctions but this can be a bit hit-and-miss.

In my experience when you have disposable income available to you and other people know that, then opportunities come to you. So look to people you like, know and trust. Make them aware you are seeking investment opportunities.

As a successful entrepreneur, almost on a daily basis I find I'm being pitched new opportunities for investment, so if you are really struggling to find something to invest in, drop me a message – office@selfmadebook.uk

Networks

That's where your networks come in. Financial advisers can provide information about investment opportunities that you might not other-wise know about. Friends and contacts can also help, if they're in the know. And for high-net-worth individuals, private banks usually pro-vide not only financial advice but also exclusive access to certain assets.

At this point you might be forgiven for saying – hold on, isn't the world full of sharks? Isn't it the case that the newspapers are crammed with stories about people who have been fleeced by advisers? And what about all those bankrupt lottery winners who were given poor advice?

Understanding your investment

Yes, these things happen, in fact are depressingly common. Whatever you consider investing in, it is absolutely critical that you understand the nature of the opportunity, what drives its value and the risks. Equally important, you need to understand the people you are dealing with. Choose advisers carefully, ideally properly qualified individuals with a track record.

And if the advice comes from friends, friends of friends or people in your network, spend time getting to know them. Who are they? What are their motivations? What do they stand to gain or lose from advising you? It's even more important to get to know potential partners – for instance, people you might be thinking of backing in a business venture or joining in a plan to redevelop a property.

We hear stories all of the time about investments going wrong with friends and family. By the very nature of investing, your money is almost never secured.

We have seen both sides. We have invested in a friend for whom our investment is now worth more than 17 times in less than 12 months. But – and this is an important caveat – we have also had situations where we thought we knew the people very well and the investment has been compromised: when times got tough, they weren't the people we expected them to be, business-wise.

We are all human and we are not infallible, so don't worry if you get it wrong. But focus on doing the best investments that you can, because fundamentally you have to be in it to win it.

Ultimately, making money work for you is not solely about investment. It is about maintaining a healthy relationship with the money you earn. Keeping track of your spending and your use of credit cards can do wonders for your sense of wellbeing. Savings and investment enable you to plan and create a better future.

The Rich Forever checklist

- Think about your relationship with money. Do you save or spend everything you earn? Are you in debt or cash positive? Do you invest? Regardless of your situation, think about why you manage money as you do.
- What lessons have you learned – good and bad – from family and friends?
- Ask yourself whether you are happy in your situation.
- What lifestyle do you aspire to? And what is 'the number'? How much do you need to earn?
- Assess you income streams. How do you earn money?
- Consider additional income streams and how you could develop them?
- Make plans to invest accordingly.
- Ask yourself how much you are prepared to lose.
- Tell people you want to invest. Offers will come your way.
- Assess all potential investments carefully.

CHAPTER THREE
Utilizing and Maximizing Your Credit Score

Suze Orman, number-one *New York Times* bestselling author and personal finance expert was quoted as saying 'I love, love, love that you want to use your debit card. But to keep your credit score solid, you still need to keep a few credit cards and use them at least once every few months' in an interview with CNN. There is a simple three-digit number that can have a significant impact on your finances, or, to be more precise, the interest you'll pay on bank loans or credit cards. I'm talking about credit scoring, the much misunderstood system used by banks and other financial institutions to assess whether individuals are 'creditworthy'.

The importance of having a good or excellent credit score is something that Byron and I became aware of very early in our money journey. What we realized was simply this: a high rating makes it easier to borrow on good terms. That in turn enables you to use debt in the right way to pursue personal and business ambitions.

So what is your credit score? Why is it important? And how can you use the system to your advantage?

A poor credit score can have a direct impact on your life. Let's take a common example, buying a mobile phone should be straightforward. You go into a store, decide on a handset that appeals to you and then find an assistant to help you complete the purchase. And, in most cases, that's exactly what happens.

But not always. Unless you're buying a phone outright with the intention of paying for your calls and data on separate monthly direct debit or a pay-as-you-go arrangement, what you'll actually be doing is entering into a credit agreement.

The store sells you the phone for a minimal upfront fee and the balance will typically be paid over 24 or 36 months, with call and data charges factored into the overall repayment costs. It's a hybrid form of hire-purchase agreement and a useful way to spread the cost of a pretty expensive item.

Except when the computer says no. In a few cases, the customer is told the required credit is not available, either on all of the displayed handsets or a few of the more expensive ones. It can be a shock to find – although they probably won't be told this quite so bluntly – that they're not considered a good risk.

Fun story

When Byron worked for Phones4U there was a major shift when they introduced a 24-month contract instead of a 12-month contract. It blew people's minds: they could not comprehend the shift in duration and became very apprehensive about proceeding with the contract and the idea of keeping one phone for more than a year. Byron laughs now, because 24 months is considered the norm. Times have definitely changed, and so has technology.

There are dozens of similar scenarios. You may be turned down for instant credit on a website. Or it could be that you apply for a loan from a bank, the application is granted but the interest quoted is higher than the 'indicative' rate that was advertised. And that last point is important. A poor credit score won't necessarily prevent you from borrowing but it can raise the cost considerably.

Behind the scenes

So why does this happen? Well, the short answer is that, before you buy goods on credit, a behind-the-scenes check will take place to establish your personal credit score. Most of the time, it's a pretty instant, and also invisible, process. The check can take place when you're in a mobile phone shop or as soon as you make an online application for a buy now pay later deal. If you call a bank to arrange a loan, the assistant may check your credit score while you're on the phone and say it's all fine. However, if the loan goes ahead and is confirmed, the bank might set a higher-than-expected interest rate according to its assessment of your creditworthiness. The higher the perceived risk, the higher the interest rate.

Your credit score plays a major role in determining how that risk is assessed, although it's not the only factor.

But what exactly are we talking about here? The term 'credit score' or 'rating' has become increasingly familiar. The companies that provide ratings – credit reference agencies such as Experian and Equifax – not only provide banks with information about potential borrowers, but also market themselves to consumers directly. So you'll see them advertising on TV and in newspapers. They may even send you emails inviting you to sign up with them and check your own credit score online.

Yet, despite all the publicity, many people don't even know they have a credit score and this lack of awareness can create real problems. Why? Because more or less everything you do within the financial system is tracked and analysed, particularly when it involves debt. If you handle borrowing badly or in a way that suggests you're being irresponsible, your rating will fall. That in turn will make you much less attractive to lenders.

Why credit scores matter

It isn't that difficult to make the kind of mistakes that will raise red flags. Think of it this way. Everywhere you go, you are offered credit in one form or another: store cards, instant credit on websites, credit cards, the list goes on. The amount of cash you borrow via any of these products may be quite small individually but with multiple sources of credit easily available, the debts can soon mount up. And here's the problem. You might forget to make a payment when it falls due. Or you might skip paying you're short of money at a particular time. You might see this as a small thing – only a missed payment – but the lender will class it as a much scarier-sounding 'default'. Even so, missing a payment deadline might not seem like such a big deal. The sky doesn't fall in and you can catch up later. Because you aren't aware you have a credit score, you carry on doing it. Before too long, your credit rating dips. One day, when you really do need to borrow money – say, to purchase a car or take out a mortgage – the low score comes back to bite you. You could well be given credit but at a higher interest rate than would otherwise be the case.

This is a trap that young people are, perhaps, particularly prone to, especially when they leave school and find they are being offered credit from all directions. A few silly decisions can store up trouble in the future. I've always believed very strongly that schools should educate students in money matters before they go out into the world. In practice, that's very often not the case.

And, in fairness, the credit score trap is seldom made clear. If you take out, say, a store card, it's in the small print that failure to make payments on time will reduce your credit score. That warning, however, often gets lost in the thrust of the marketing message. The lenders want your business because the interest you pay is how they make their money. So, they will naturally accentuate the positive by extolling the benefits of buying now and paying later as a means to manage outgoings. The downside is hidden away somewhere.

No debt is also a problem

So if too much debt is a problem, then you might assume that no debt at all is a major positive.

That's not actually the case. If you've never taken out any kind of credit, you could find it difficult to access a bank loan or a car deal.

Credit reference agencies assess your creditworthiness by tracking how you manage your debt. If you've never had a store card, or a credit card, then in data terms you are a blank sheet. They don't know who you are and they can't provide a rating.

Ironically, you can be the most responsible person imaginable – living within your means and handling money really well – and yet be turned down for a mobile phone because you have no debt history. This has even happened to well-paid celebrities who previously had had no need for credit.

So I would invite you to think about who you are for a second. Are you the person who has always refused the opportunity to acquire a credit card, thinking that it is better to pay in cash? Or have you seized all the opportunities to finesse your monthly finances by using various forms of credit? And if you are that second kind of person, have you occasionally struggled to meet the repayments or failed to meet one of the monthly deadlines?

The truth is: there's a balance, a sunlit middle ground between the two scenarios I've just outlined. It's important to understand how to correctly strike that balance.

How the system works

The credit score system is cloaked in a certain amount of mystery. You'll often be told, for instance, that even applying unsuccessfully for credit can push down your rating. And, of course, missed payments have the same effect. But why?

So let's talk about how the system works.

Starting with the basics, the credit score is the primary means by which lenders decide whether you are a good risk. Or, to put it another way, it is how they satisfy themselves that you are in the best possible position to repay the money you have borrowed in a timely and regular way. Often that repayment will be monthly. It's not the only method. Banks run their own checks in addition to the credit score. It is, however, the open sesame for many credit offers.

The credit score is based on data that is pooled by a range of credit providers. These not only include banks, credit card providers and store card operators but also mobile phone companies and utilities. Yes, if you pay your gas and electricity bills by direct debit in arrears of actually using the energy, you are accessing credit. Generally speaking, government data, such as local tax payment records, are not fed into the system. At least that's the situation here in the UK.

A credit score is usually rendered as a three-digit number. A high score means you will not only be able to access credit but you will also (probably) be offered good deals. In the case of a really low score, you may struggle to get any kind of credit at all but most likely you will be offered something but at a high cost.

What is a good score?

To take an example. In the case of Experian, the best score is 999 but anywhere between 881 and 960 is considered good. Fair to average is 721 to 880. Below that is poor or very poor. On Equifax the highest score is 700. At first glance, the scores might seem difficult to interpret, but you can easily find your current score and what it means in practice by using the free services supplied by the various credit reference agencies.

All you need to do is go to one of their websites and open an account. You will have to provide a few details, including, naturally enough, your name and address. The agencies will require verification of your identity, and in the UK this particular check is linked to your presence on the electoral register. You may also be asked for your previous address, plus your landline and mobile numbers. Depending on the company, some other ID may be required for verification.

In the USA, aside from name and address details, the most important piece of information is the Primary Account Number (PAN). Essentially, this is the number of the first bank (or financial institution) account opened by the individual.

It's a fairly instant process. Whether you know it or not, you already have a credit score. All the rating company has to do is retrieve the figure from its system based on your details.

You can also use the system to review your finances in terms of open accounts and whether or not financial institutions have been searching through your details. I'll be talking more about that later.

You may also be shown details of card companies and loan providers that offer credit appropriate to your score. So, in addition to being told that your rating is excellent, poor or somewhere in between, you can consider appropriate finance products.

Why do the ratings agencies offer this additional service? Well, unsurprisingly they earn commissions when a consumer successfully applies for a card or a loan, so it's in their interest to match the right score with an appropriate deal.

You might be surprised by your score, either because it's higher than you expected or lower. That raises the question of how the rating was arrived at. There are a number of factors that are taken into consideration.

How your rating is arrived at

A hefty 35 per cent of the credit score is based on an analysis of your payment history, or, to put it more bluntly, your record of paying on time. This is why it's really important not to default on credit or store cards, or indeed to cancel direct debits without agreement. On the plus side, making a point of paying on time helps maintain or boost your score. You can make sure you do so by setting up a direct debit rather than just transferring cash on an ad hoc basis when the payment falls due.

The repayment history data cover a wide range of borrowing activity. For instance, many people don't really consider their mobile phone bill as being part of a credit profile. But it is, and missing a bill payment will affect your rating.

Then there is the total amount owed. This represents 30 per cent of the total score. Lenders are quite keen on approving credit deals, but they also want to ensure that customers are not overstretched. So the credit reference agencies will look at how much an individual is already borrowing and how the debt breaks down across various lines of credit. For instance, they will look at whether you are permanently maxed out on one or more credit cards. If so, this might suggest you don't have the ability to reduce the debt or manage the card well. Again, this is reflected in the rating.

New debt can affect your score. For instance, if you take out a fresh loan, there will be no record how regularly you are making payments. Until a payment record is established, your credit score might fall. This should, however, be temporary.

This can be galling. Byron saw his score drop temporarily after he applied for a credit card, and knowing the importance of remaining at 999 he was determined to get back to the top rating as quickly as possible. I have to say there was a bit of competition between us on credit scores for a while.

There is a bigger point here. While it's great to have the highest credit score, it won't actually do you much good unless you are using credit. Credit is, after all, there to be used. Applying for credit may push your score down for a while but by continuing to use debt sensibly, it can quickly be restored.

A long-established history of using credit – provided you've done so responsibly – should give your credit score a boost. This is quite logical. If a borrower has a history stretching back just a couple of years, the ratings companies have relatively little data to go on. Someone with a 30-year record, on the other hand, is a data rich prospect. Generally speaking, the longer the history, the less risky you are considered. This aspect represents 15 per cent of the rating.

The type of credit you access is also a factor. Using a range of debt options can be a good thing. If handled responsibly, a mix that includes bank loans, credit cards, a car loan and a mortgage would positively influence your score and this factor represents 10 per cent of the total.

But there's a caveat. A rush of new activity across a range of different loans can be a red flag to the agencies and the lenders. For instance, if you are maxed out on two credit cards and apply for a third, that can be an indication that you're struggling to make ends meet.

Credit utilization

All of which brings to the subject of credit utilization, or how you actually manage your borrowing.

Your utilization rate is worked out by agencies on the basis of what you're borrowing from so-called revolving sources of credit, such as credit cards.

There's a bit of industry jargon to explain here. Revolving credit refers to a borrowing option that is automatically renewed. A bank loan is not revolving credit because once all the payments are made, it falls away. If you want more money, you have to take out another loan. A credit card, on the other hand, is there when you need it on an ongoing basis. But, compared to a loan, it's also very expensive.

Your credit utilization rate is worked out by dividing the amount of revolving borrowing you have at any one time by the total amount of credit available to you. Thus, if you have two cards, each with a limit of £10,000, your available credit is £20,000. If you have £5,000 borrowed then your utilization rate is 25 percent. If £10,000 is the sum borrowed, the rate is 50 per cent.

A high utilization rate also affects how you are perceived. Experian says utilization rates influence up to 30 percent of your credit score. From that perspective, it's a good idea to keep your rate below 25. Lenders will say 25 to 30 per cent, but I would err on the side of caution.

So, if your available credit is £4,000, don't go above £1,000 at any one time.

But frankly, the lower the better. Ideally, we would all treat credit cards almost like debit cards. Let's say you spend £200 on your card in a month and repay that sum in full when it comes due. This is not only good for utilization rate but is also positive for your bank account. Credit card annual interest rates are high, but if you pay off the debt immediately – or to be more precise at the next payment deadline – you avoid interest entirely. After that, the faster you pay off the debt, the less interest you pay.

This takes us into the flexible world of APR, standing for annualized percentage rate. The APR on a credit card might be 20 per cent, which is high by loan standards. But that's the figure if the debt is cleared in a year. Pay off in a month and the interest amounts to just one-twelfth of that.

On expensive items spreading the payments over a year or more makes a huge difference to overall costs. And if there are a lot of purchases on the card, all being paid off over a protracted timeframe, the cumulative interest makes the total debt much harder to deal with.

If you're in that situation, the best solution is to transfer the balance to a new card – one that offers 0 per cent interest for a number of months. This will allow you to wipe out what you owe with no additional interest accruing. The 0 interest period may only last six months or a year. If you haven't paid the debt by then, transfer to a new card. A strong credit score will stand you in good stead when you're applying for new cards. And it's a virtuous circle. By clearing the debt quickly, you'll reduce the credit utilization rate. Result – a rating boost.

Paying off any credit card debt you owe ahead of the monthly deadline can also bump up the score.

It's a bit of a game really, and like any sporting activity, you're going to fare better if you know the rules. It's a bit like being a striker in a soccer team. If you fully understand the offside rule, you'll score more goals. If you don't, the referee will be constantly blowing the whistle.

Up against the limit

Finally, it's worth thinking about your credit limit. There are a couple of points to make here. By applying for a higher ceiling, you can actually lower your utilization rate, simply because you change the equation between the money you owe and the amount you can borrow. Another example of how it's possible to game the system to your benefit.

I would suggest, however, that you don't ask for a higher limit within six months of applying for a card. As far as the credit reference agency computer algorithms are concerned, this suggests you are struggling to make ends meet or just too keen to take on a lot of revolving debt.

In my view, the limit should align with your salary. It doesn't make sense to have a borrowing facility that is well beyond your ability to make repayments.

Check your score regularly

Once you've checked on your credit score for the first time, it's a good idea to keep on doing it on a regular basis. To be honest, the reference agency that you've opened an account with will probably advise you to do that every month or so, usually via email.

So, why check it again? Let's assume you have the best possible score. That's great, you can rest assured that you're doing everything right.

You probably are, but things can change. Sometimes that's because of what you're doing today rather than six months ago. If your financial behaviours change, your score could dip. If that's the case, then it's good to know because you can take action to restore it.

However, a sudden movement could also mean that something more worrying is happening. We live in an age where everything is digitized and you can access credit relatively easily online without going anywhere near a bank. That's convenient but also a bit dangerous. No matter how careful you are, there is always the potential to fall victim to identity theft. A criminal finds out enough about you – and this can be done in large part through social media – to open accounts in your name.

One useful function of checking a credit score is that it can flag unusual activity, allowing you to identify fraud and take action.

For instance, your credit report provides information on accounts you're linked to. If any of these are unfamiliar, it's a sign a fraudster may have opened one or more in your name. Equally important, credit reports also contain information about lenders that have scanned your details. This really only happens when you apply for credit. If you haven't applied for credit but your file has been searched, there is a chance that someone is considering opening a fraudulent account. If so, inform the lender and the reference agency.

Soft and hard searches

What I should stress is that searches of your credit history are not in themselves sinister. They take place every time that you apply for credit.

But they can be a cause for some concern even when fraudsters aren't involved. An unsuccessful credit application can downwardly impact your score. This fact alone deters some people from researching their credit options, so it's important to understand the ground rules.

There are two types of searches – hard and soft.

If you are using a comparison platform to compare insurance, the site will do a **soft search**. Really the website is just checking that you are, indeed, who you say you are and that you can – based on the data – afford to pay any instalments. A soft search doesn't appear on your credit file, and it won't affect your credit score.

A **hard search** is more rigorous. If you apply for a loan, credit card or mortgage, the lender will do a deep dive into your credit history, looking at all your accounts and your repayment records. This kind of search does appear on your credit file, and in some circumstances it might affect the rating, especially if the application is ultimately rejected.

If you are going to trigger a lot of searches, I would suggest doing them all at once rather than separately over a longer period of time. This suggests to the system you are making comparisons between providers in a calculated way rather than constantly seeking to access new borrowing products.

County court judgements

As I mentioned before, credit reference agencies don't collect data from local councils or indeed from most private companies.

But that doesn't mean that you can fail to pay a parking ticket, build up arrears on council tax, or neglect to honour an invoice from a local company with impunity. Late payment won't be reported to the bank, but a successful legal action resulting in a court judgement will definitely affect your credit score in a major way.

It works like this. Let's say you don't pay a bill. There may be a good reason for this. Perhaps you're in dispute with someone who has carried out a service on your behalf. You say the job was not done well and refuse to pay. The supplier takes the case to a court and wins. The result is a judgement against your name.

In the UK this is known as a county court judgement, and it will stay on your file for six long years unless you pay within 30 days. According to Registry Trust Ltd, which holds data on such judgements, the number of registered judgements in 2022 was 899,257. There are similar systems in other countries.

You really shouldn't get to that situation. One thing that happens all the time is that a case is taken to a court and documentation is sent out to the alleged debtor. For whatever reason, the recipient of the documents doesn't reply to the court. This is designated a 'failure to respond'. If this happens, the case – regardless of the rights and wrongs – will be settled in favour of the complainant. It's automatic.

So, if you find yourself in this situation, the first rule is don't bury your head in the sand. The court proceedings won't go away because you choose to ignore them.

If a judgement does go against you, there are two ways to deal with it.

First, you could reach out to the court and ask to have the judgement set aside. You'll have to make a case for this, explaining why you didn't or couldn't respond to the court documents. For instance, you may have been unaware of the proceedings. Equally important, the court will ask for evidence that you don't actually owe the money. There may be a court fee, even if you succeed.

Alternatively, you can contact the lender or creditor and ask to have the judgement set aside as a term of the settlement.

Case study: Chloe

Byron has a friend named Chloe (we've changed her name to protect her privacy) who came to him as she had received a county court judgement as a result of an unpaid parking ticket. While this may seem to be a very specific circumstance, legal problems arising from unpaid fines are common. In fact, Byron has been asked for help with similar problems on many occasions. The issue was this. The parking ticket and the consequent court judgement resulted in Chloe being refused for credit no matter where she turned. Lenders don't like court judgements. But there was a solution. Byron made a request to the court to set aside the county court judgement on the grounds that was not only unfairly placed but also didn't follow protocol. The objective was not to resolve the issue of the parking ticket but to have the court judgement removed from her file. As mentioned before, satisfying the file would have meant it would have remained on Chloe's credit report for six years. Before the court date was set, the claimant decided to provide a draft order agreeing to remove the judgement. Chloe has now gone on to use her credit in multiple ways to satisfy her and her family's lifestyle which included being able to purchase her first home.

For more information, we have set up a website: https://thecreditscorefix.uk/ The site provides both information and all the legal templates you are likely to need when dealing with a judgement.

Really, you never want to receive a county court judgement. You want to do everything in your power to avoid it. So this means paying your parking tickets and bills promptly, or in the case of parking tickets and other fines avoiding them in the first place!

The same is true of being flagged by banks as a potential fraudster. Here in the UK, a voluntary body known as the Credit Industry Fraud Avoidance System (CIFAS) collects data on individuals. The organization can place a flag indicating fraud (a CIFAS marker) against an individual's name. Unless it is removed, that person could find it impossible to access credit. In the USA, the Department of Justice encourages banks to share data on suspected fraud.

Now, fraud is a big word conjuring images of dangerous criminals. But you can get a CIFAS marker for something as simple as amending a bank statement. People do this all the time but that doesn't mean it won't be taken seriously by lenders. So don't do it. Don't do anything to misrepresent your financial status to gain credit. It is bad news.

You can get a CIFAS marker removed. To do that, you will first need to understand why you were flagged and you may be able to make a case that the lender has acted unreasonably. If that fails, then you can have a conversation with the lender. You could also ask CIFAS to investigate with a view to removal. Again, there is advice on this on our https://thecreditscorefix.uk website.

Watching your allies

The word 'allies' is generally considered to have positive connotations. Allies are our friends or people who help us. Having allies is good.

Or maybe not. From a financial services perspective, allies can be a problem. They are people you are linked to financially. For instance, you may have a joint account with a business partner or a spouse.

The credit score of an ally can affect your rating. So be very careful about who you are associated with financially.

The Rich Forever checklist

- If you haven't done so already, find a credit reference agency and check your score.
- While you're doing that, check that all the information is correct, including account details, home address and phone numbers.
- Check that there is no activity on the credit file that could be cause for concern – for instance, accounts you don't recognize or erroneous searches that are not linked to your own activity. If so, make sure these details are removed.
- If there is any indication of fraud, make sure you report it and that it is investigated.
- So let's assume everything is OK. Then you have a great opportunity to review your finances. Analyse where you have outstanding debt. Consider your current state of play

---

and how it can be improved. As an exercise, take note of your score and take steps to improve it. This may involve a change of mindset around how you handle debt.

- Check your credit score on a monthly basis to ensure it reflects the current state of play. In terms of good housekeeping, set up an automatic direct debit for your cards at the end of each month, perhaps ahead of the issuer's deadline.
- Remove any financial allies that are no longer current.
- Keep credit card debt to 25 per cent of the total credit limit (across all cards)
- Bonus tip: PAY YOUR BILLS ON TIME!

In short, take control of your credit future.

Now, you've improved your credit score. Let's talk about how to get out of debt and use your credit score to utilize debt in your journey to being rich forever!

CHAPTER FOUR
Getting out of Debt and Using Debt the Right Way

Debt. It can drag you down and, quite frankly, make your life a misery but that's by no means the whole picture. As accurately described by Robert Kiyosaki, author of *Rich Dad, Poor Dad*, 'Good debt is a powerful tool, but bad debt can kill you.' Most of us borrow money at some time in our lives, even if it's only to purchase a car or buy a house. And debt can be an enabler for many positive and constructive things. It can fund your education, finance the purchase of an investment property or provide a business with the working capital needed to expand and ultimately increase its profits.

Both Bianca and I have used debt positively to invest in ourselves and grow our businesses.

In other words, borrowing can be a very good thing in the right circumstances. It's not something to be afraid of. On the other hand, you need to understand the difference between bad and good debt. The former is best avoided. The latter can help you achieve your financial goals.

Households in Britain had debts averaging £65,000 in 2022, according to figures published by the Money Charity. Within that figure, credit card debt averaged £2,290. Total unsecured debt – money lent without any claim on assets – averaged £3,914. Overall debt in the UK amounts to £1.28 trillion.

It's a similar picture in the USA. According to credit rating agency Experian, the average American owed $101,000 in 2022, but the total sum quoted disguises a lot of variation. Some of that debt was accounted for by mortgages, which averaged out at more than $200,000 and there was also high borrowing on student loans and cars. Credit card debt averaged $5,910.

Those figures tell a story. When you dig beneath the surface, you find a huge amount of variation in the way that people borrow and the impact – both positive and negative – of the debt they have accrued.

For instance, mortgages represent not only a long-term debt – repayable over perhaps 20 or 30 years – but also a means to secure ownership of an appreciating asset. Monthly payments can draw off a high percentage of monthly income, but most of those who buy property in this way feel pretty good about it. They have borrowed with a purpose.

At the other end of the spectrum, credit and store cards provide rapid access to money and flexible repayments. The convenience and flexibility of credit cards can be extremely useful but the associated debts can mount up over time and become unmanageable. According to the charity Debt Justice, about 10 million people in Britain are in serious financial difficulty because of the money they owe. In that respect, a credit card can be both good and bad. It really depends on how you use your plastic and what the money is spent on.

So that raises questions not just about how to borrow but also when and why it might be a good or bad idea to take advantage of the credit that is widely available to most of us. When it comes to debt, what is good and bad?

Bad debt

So let's start by taking a look at the kind of borrowing you should – if at all humanly possible – avoid.

Broadly speaking, it is not a good idea to get into debt to pay for goods and services that have no value to you over the longer term. This is particularly true if you find yourself making repayments over months and years for items that are either worthless or valued at a fraction of what you paid. It's probably fine to use a credit card to pay for a dream holiday if you can genuinely pay the money back over two or three months. But if you're still paying it off a year or two later, it's a different equation. The benefits of the holiday are half forgotten but the debt burden is still there. Meanwhile, the card is probably being used for other purchases as well. So there's a potential for things to get out of control.

The same principle applies to all forms of flexible, high-interest credit. Payday loans are a case in point. The payday loans industry has declined following an influx of bad publicity, but it is still possible to access high-interest, short-term finance. The target customer is someone who needs money to solve an immediate problem such as paying a bill or buying groceries, maybe towards the end of the month when resources are at their lowest. The loan provides instant cash and low interest if the debt is repaid quickly. In that respect, you could argue that such loans serve a purpose. But I would say: be very careful. The annual percentage rate (APR) is usually very high.

In practice, that means the longer the repayment period the more crippling the interest burden becomes. There's a further problem. If a borrower is already strapped for cash the loan repayment just sucks away more disposable income. The likelihood is that more borrowed money will be required as the weeks pass, with rapid repayment becoming impossible. Debts build up.

The same scenario can arise with 'buy now, pay later' buttons on websites and store cards. And, sadly, there are still loan sharks out there, typically lending money in disadvantaged communities.

Now borrowing on flexible terms and repaying over a period of months isn't always bad. It could be, for example, that a credit card is the best way to pay for tools (that will earn you money) or a college course. But, in these cases, you'll have something to show when making the repayments. What you don't want to do it saddle yourself with a long-term liability for no good reason.

Equally, a card can be a liquidity tool. It may be that, even with a high interest rate, a card provides the best way to spread payments over a six-month period while keeping cash in your bank account.

But you need to think about whether it's the right option. I'll be talking more about liquidity later in the chapter.

And if you are an impulse buyer – someone who sees a Louis Vuitton bag in a shop and simply has to have it – then a credit card is probably not for you.

Buying a car

There are certain purchases that you might think will be around for a while – a new car, for instance, purchased via a three-year lease-hire deal or something similar. That's something solid, isn't it?

Actually, it's a depreciating asset. It's not always a good idea to commit yourself to big monthly repayments for something that loses value with every day that passes.

So by all means buy a car. You may well need one, but does it really need to be a Benz costing £600 or more a month if you really can't afford to make the payments? Yes, you may feel good as you drive through your local area at the wheel of an iconic vehicle. But that feeling is likely to wear off very quickly if you are struggling to pay bills.

So be realistic about your financial circumstances and avoid over-reaching yourself for a short-term and fleeting burst of ownership satisfaction.

The truth is that crippling yourself with debt won't necessarily enhance your life, even if that Benz is sitting outside your house or apartment. At times it is better to get a car that gets you around affordably. That doesn't mean denying yourself. My first car was an M-reg Vauxhall Corsa and I loved it. Bianca felt equally warmly about her first vehicle, a Renault Clio. It's a question of staying in your lane.

That doesn't mean you'll always drive an M-reg Corsa. It's really a question of what you can afford and where your life and career are sitting at any particular moment. We all know that cars depreciate in value, but there are times when it makes sense to buy something expensive. For instance, Bianca and I drive luxury cars and that's part of our business. It's something I make money from.

Getting out of bad debt

So what do you do when debt becomes a problem – small, large or overwhelming?

It's all too easy to make purchases on a credit card, defer the repayment and then make some more. Before long you're paying for multiple items bought over time and never fully paid for. The monthly payments become hard to service. Sitting alongside the bills that may also be piling up, debt is starting to dominate your life.

Debt can destroy relationships. According to TD Ameritrade, around 41 per cent of divorcees from the Generation X cohort and 29 per cent of baby boomers ended their marriages because of money problems. When debt gets out of hand, it can be seriously corrosive.

It can also be bad for your health. Debt leads to anxiety and depression. A UK study by the Royal College of Psychiatrists found that half of people with debt problems also struggle with mental health. And it can be a vicious circle. Mental health issues make it harder to manage money, making it more likely that debt will become a problem. This in turn feeds back onto worsening mental health. All this may manifest as physical symptoms, such as headaches, fatigue and even heart problems.

So, how do you rid yourself of the burden of debt?

Acknowledging the problem

The first step is to acknowledge that you are actually in debt. Now, I'm not really talking about the mortgage that is part of your monthly budget or even paying an affordable sum every month to the credit card company. What you have to acknowledge is that you have a debt that you want (or need) to clear.

That can be tough. It perhaps also means acknowledging you could have handled your financial affairs a bit better. Even more difficult, you're accepting there is some kind of a problem that has to be addressed. So be honest with yourself.

And also with those you love. If you're in a long-term relationship or have a family, the debts you've accrued will affect others as well. Part of acknowledging the problem is being prepared to talk to others who are affected.

Then think about the why. If you're going to make a concerted effort to bring down your borrowing, it probably isn't enough to say, 'I want to clear my debts.' You will be much more successful if you give yourself solid reasons.

For instance, the level of debt might be fuelling anxiety. Even if the monthly payments are affordable, they may seem like a burden if you also feel insecure financially, perhaps because of unstable employment or an underperforming business. More positively, it could be that reducing debt will boost disposable income. Having fewer bills to pay each month feeds through to having more spending money.

Paying off debts quickly should also improve your credit score. That will make it cheaper to access finance when you really need it to do something that will positively affect your life.

Then there is the question of household culture. It probably isn't a good idea to bring children up in a household in which parents are stressed out by debt. Living demonstrably within your means teaches children good habits.

Making a plan

Once you've pinned down your reasons, you're going to need three things, namely:

- a plan
- a budget
- a timeframe.

A timeframe gives you something to work to and may be linked to a life event. You want to clear your debts before quitting work to start a business in a year's time. Or your goal is to get down to zero before you retire. Alternatively, you could simply decide on a timeframe that suits you.

The budget looks at how you're going to pay off what you owe over that allotted period. It's not just a case of how much is allocated for repayments. It's also important to chart the totality of money coming in and out.

This is closely related to the plan. Exactly how are you going to achieve your ambition?

Budgeting

Start by tracking your budget. What are you spending every month? It may be that you can actually spend less on certain items. So here's the good news. A great many bills are negotiable when contracts come up for renewal. For instance, if an insurer raises the cost of your home and contents or car policy, you can ring up and ask to cancel. Very often, rather than losing your business, they will offer a price that matches that of cheaper competitors. Failing that, you can cancel and use a comparison website to get a better offer. The same principle applies to mobile, broadband and utility providers.

It's worth spending a day finding out when all your contracts come to an end. Put them in the diary with a view to renegotiation.

Equally important, go through your direct debits and find subscriptions that you no longer need or use but have somehow forgotten to cancel.

In other words, you are rebalancing your budget. By spending less on some things, you are freeing up cash which can be spent elsewhere.

Boosting your income

One of the best ways to clear debt is to increase income. Now I know that isn't always easy. Going along to an employer and asking for an above-inflation pay rise is likely to evoke a sharp response, unless you are so valuable to the company that you can dictate terms.

But there are things you can do. Apply for another job. If you're in work already and a new employer wants to bring you on board, it's normal to offer a premium on your current salary as an incentive. Or you can simply apply for jobs that are – as advertised – better paid.

There could also be opportunities to work overtime or perhaps take a second job a few evenings a week.

If you work for yourself or run a company, then it's worth looking at ways to increase sales or cut costs to boost profits. If you don't already own a business, you could start a side hustle. All of these things are open to you.

In other words, it's not all about cutting back.

Setting priorities

Let's assume for a moment, your plan is purely and simply to clear all your debts as quickly as possible. In an ideal world, you would work out the budget, and allocate money to be repaid every month in order to reach zero according to a timeframe.

It may not be as simple as that. For one thing, many people have multiple debts – term loans, store cards, credit cards, car leasing deals … It's all debt but each line of credit has different characteristics. The term loan could have an APR of 8 or 9 per cent. In the case of a credit card it could be 25–26 per cent. And while the term loan has fixed repayments every month and an end date, your credit card rolls over, and unless the outstanding balance is paid in full at some clearly defined point, the debt and associated interest rates will continue to the end of time – or until the card issuer pulls the plug.

This can be something of a conundrum. Credit card debt in particular can be reduced rapidly because you can choose how much to pay each month. But what if you have three cards, a store account and a term loan (which may also allow for early repayment)? You could up the payments on all of them, of course, but that might not be affordable.

One strategy is to take out a consolidation loan. This involves taking out a term loan over maybe five or six years. This is used to pay off all the other debts, including cards. Ideally, you should be able to reduce your monthly repayment because you're consolidating high-interest card balances into one relatively low-interest term loan.

Advantages and disadvantages of debt consolidation

Think carefully. Consolidation loans can be a good solution but only if the numbers add up. For one thing, it will tie you into a fixed monthly repayments, whereas credit cards are more flexible. What's more, if you carry on spending on credit cards, you might simply end up with more debt plus a consolidation loan.

Advantages of debt consolidation:

- Simplified payments
- Lower interest rates
- Improved credit score in the long term
- Reduced stress
- Fixed repayment schedule

Disadvantages of debt consolidation:

- Potential for higher overall cost
- Risk of further debt
- Upfront fees and costs
- Potential negative impact on credit score in the short term

So when you talk to your bank about consolidation, work out whether there is more or less to pay and over what timescale and whether you can also kick the credit card habit to avoid simply creating another problem.

In the case of credit cards, another alternative is to apply for a zero-interest card and transfer any existing borrowing. During the interest-free period, you can pay down the debt without any further interest accruing. This is another form of consolidation.

The alternative to consolidation may be to prioritize – for instance, by making a real effort to pay off one loan or card completely. Once this has been done, the other monthly bills will feel more manageable and you can decide on further priorities.

So you might decide to focus on the largest debt with the highest interest rate. Or the debt that is currently requiring the biggest monthly repayment. It's about assessing the strategy that will deliver the greatest boost to your financial circumstances.

My advice would be to be as pragmatic as possible. It might be tempting to pay the smallest debt first as a way of showing yourself that you can make a rapid dent in the problem. That might be the best course of action in some circumstances. But really you want to focus on the debts that are having the biggest adverse effect on you in terms of monthly payments and the longevity of the problem. Look unemotionally at your financial situation and focus on the biggest wins.

Getting help

There are times when you might need help. That could be as simple as talking to other members of the family about what they can do – such as making an effort to reduce monthly outgoings.

But not all debt is manageable. There are times when the best course of action is to speak to a professional.

That can be a tough step. Picking up the phone or sending an email to a debt adviser really does involve acknowledging a problem. But here's the thing. A professional will be able to look at the situation with forensic clarity and come up with solutions. It's hard to make good choices in the middle of a crisis. An adviser will look unemotionally at your problem and come up with solutions.

Communication is key

In Chapter 8, 'Keeping Your Love Life', in our second book, *The Business Survival Kit*, we provide great detail around the tools needed to discuss your financial struggles with your romantic partner. Communication is key to getting the help and support that you need.

Good debt

So, if that's bad debt, what constitutes good debt? What does that look like?

As I pointed out earlier, borrowing for the right purposes can enhance your life while also enabling you to grow your wealth. That will come as news to a lot of people. Culturally, speaking there is a fear of debt within many communities. Grandparents and parents will warn their children against borrowing. It is seen as a burden.

And yet if you look at the world from the perspective of a billionaire – if you adopt that mindset – things begin to look different. In fact, debt can be used to fund investments which in turn generate income. Billionaires – and indeed millionaires – have mastered the art of using other people's money to fund their income-generating activities.

Personal development

At its foundation, you can define good debt in terms of investing in yourself. It's about borrowing to buy goods, services or assets that will make your life better in a sustained way. For instance, investing in a course that will enhance your career makes you much more valuable in the marketplace. So your income rises and the amount of money you make exceeds the principal sum and interest on the loan. For instance, I might invest in education or mentoring that will make me a better salesman. Consequently, I close more sales. I've borrowed money to make money.

I would say that investing in yourself in this way is incredibly positive form of debt. The knowledge you acquire will be there to help you forever.

Investing in knowledge

Investing in knowledge and education can cost very little – hundreds of pounds or dollars maybe or a few thousand – and depending on your circumstances, the simplest thing might be to put it on a credit card or take out a bank loan. It's an investment.

As an example, many of our mentees have managed to turn their annual income into their monthly income as a result of investing in our support. Some had with little more than an idea when they came to us and are now millionaires.

Student loans

Student debt is different. Here in the UK, tuition fees are currently set at a maximum level of just over £9,000 a year and most universities do charge the full allowable amount. To do otherwise, would a) deprive them of revenue and b) suggest their courses were somehow cut price. Loans are available both for tuition fees and for living costs. It's very common to finish a degree with debts of more than £40,000. Overseas students pay more. In the USA, there is more variation in fees depending on the university and whether it is public or private, but the story is the same. Unless you have alternative funds available, going to university often involves borrowing. The terms of loan repayments vary according to country.

The repayment terms can be benign. In the UK, student debt repayments are managed by the Student Loans Company and collected by the tax authority with the amount payable monthly being linked to income. Low earners pay nothing at all. Currently, any money that isn't repaid after 30 years is written off, although that could change.

So is it worth it? Certainly, if you're pursuing a career that requires a formal education – professions like medicine, dentistry, the law or teaching – it absolutely is.

On the other hand, there are a lot of career paths that don't require degree-level education. Apple founder Steve Jobs, Facebook supremo, Mark Zuckerberg, and Michael Dell of Dell Computers fame and many other seasoned and successful entrepreneurs are famously college dropouts. Richard Branson never went to university. In the USA a surprisingly high percentage of students – 40 per cent, according to Think Impact – quit their courses. In the UK, the dropout rate is much lower, at 6.4 per cent.

There are a few things to think about:

- Could you pursue your chosen career more or equally successfully without a degree?
- If you're not absolutely sure that university is right for you, is there a risk of not completing the course but still having quite a lot of debt to repay?
- Is it the right course for you?
- Is university the best route?

The answer to those questions is very much down to each and every individual.

Is student debt good or bad?

I going to try my best to not sit on the fence on this. By and large, student debt is good debt, as long as you are certain going to university is what you want to do. It's also important to remember that the benefits of university go beyond the courses themselves. You make lifelong friends and build networks.

However, as an entrepreneur who has studied for a business and economics degree, I question how practical the information and skills I acquired were when it came to the real world.

Investing in a business

Investing in a business is another good use of debt. Not every new business requires a lot of capital, but there will generally be a gap of weeks or months between the moment the shutters (metaphorical or otherwise) open on the new venture and the day when sales are generating enough money to live on and meet all the costs of trading.

There are various ways of funding a new business through debt. In the early days of our respective business careers, both Bianca and I used credit cards to pay for essentials and live day-to-day. I used my Capital One card. It's not really what they were designed to do, but they provide flexible credit when you need it.

Other forms of credit include business loans – repayable over an agreed period – and invoice financing (also known as invoice factoring). The latter is a kind of rolling credit. If a business delivers a service and invoices the customer, payment can take a month or more to come through, creating a cash void. An invoice discounter lends against the value of outstanding invoices. Essentially, this means the business gets the cash related to a sale as soon as a bill is sent.

So you choose the type of debt accordingly. Maybe a credit card is useful to keep you going in the early stages. A long-term debt can provide capital to grow the business. Borrowing against invoices helps with cashflow management.

There is a cost to all of these arrangements, but they enable businesses to acquire customers, manage cash flow and make profits. In the case of successful companies debt is a good investment. Again, ultimately you get more money back than you've paid to the lender.

The caveat is that all debt comes with the risk that repayment could be difficult and ultimately your business could fail. Even if this is the case, the lessons learned from the experience will prepare you for your next possible venture. As I like to say: 'It may be your first business, but for most people it may not be the last.'

Mortgages and property

Taking out a mortgage may be one of the best investments you ever make. If your goal is to secure a place to live, a mortgage helps you achieve that aim while also providing an asset that history suggests will increase in value. Within a matter of years, the house or apartment is likely to be worth significantly more than you paid for it. Wait a few years longer and the monthly repayments won't seem so onerous. As your income grows, the repayments – give or take interest fluctuations – remain relatively fixed.

There is a debate around this. Robert Kiyosaki, author of *Rich Dad, Poor Dad*, argues that buying a property to live in is a bad debt because it takes money out of his bank account. Whilst we understand the concept and enjoy some of his teachings, we disagree.

It's a personal choice, but buying a property to provide rental income is definitely good debt. Typically, the rent you charge covers the mortgage with profit on top. And, again, you have an appreciating asset to sell at a chosen time. Buying to let has the advantage of delivering passive income. The money comes in every month with minimum effort on your part.

> **Example**
>
> If the average property price in the UK is £295,000 and you have £75,000 in your bank account. You use that money as a deposit to buy a property that will require a £650 per month mortgage. The rental is £1,150 a month, so that's £500 in profit. That in itself is not life-changing, but the arrangement means you are earning money while watching the value of the asset rise.

Buying property has been a hugely important part of my financial story.

Other investments

The same can be said of other forms of investment. You can borrow to fund investments that deliver a return. To take an example, many stocks and shares platforms accept credit card payment. So, you can use your card of choice to pay the required deposit and then begin trading.

The important thing is to use debt to invest in assets that have a good chance of providing a return that is over and above the cost of servicing the loan. It can be applied to a whole range of investment opportunities from antiques and wine to bonds.

Other people's money – the magic of leverage

All of this brings us to the important topic of leverage. This is a term that you often hear on the TV or radio when a big takeover deal is being announced. For instance, you might hear that a football club has been acquired through a leveraged buyout.

All this means is that the buyer has bought the club using borrowed money. Usually, in this kind of arrangement, the business that has been acquired is also responsible for paying the debt that funded its own acquisition.

For buyers, that is an incredibly good arrangement. They can purchase an asset without dipping too far into their own funds. Instead, the asset itself pays for itself.

More generally, financial leverage means using borrowed money to fund the acquisition of an asset and amplify returns.

Leverage is not just for big corporations. Anyone who can access credit can take advantage of the concept.

Perhaps the best example is buying property to rent out. In 2006, I borrowed £130,000 to buy a maisonette (duplex). My own outlay was minimal as most of the money was borrowed. It would be worth £400,000 today.

Now, that seems like an obvious thing to do, but not everybody gets it. In fact, a friend tried to talk me out of it, saying, 'Why do that?' I didn't listen. I went ahead and bought it because borrowing enabled me to invest and secure a return.

By using leverage you can become like a bank. Think of it this way: banks operate – at least in part – by taking money from savers and using the cash to invest in assets and projects that will deliver profits. Savers are protected because there are strict rules about how much of their money – in percentage terms – can be reinvested at any one time. The bank benefits because it makes a profit. Savers enjoy a return on their capital.

Leverage works in exactly the same way. You take someone else's money. Invest it. The returns benefit both you and the lender. It can seem like high finance, but the concept is very simple.

Is there a catch? Only that you need to know what you're doing. Or, to put it another way, if leverage is to work for you, it's important to have a system.

In practice, that means, first and foremost, identifying a proven money-making vehicle. That could be buying a house to rent out, using borrowed money to invest in stocks and shares or buying a business. However, the key is to find an asset that will give you an income higher than the amount you are required to repay. This is a golden rule.

So it follows you have to think about the source of the funding. How much will the money cost and over what period? Understanding the terms and implications of the loan is a vital part of building a system of leverage that adds up.

A property system would look something like this:

1 Find the property.
2 Source the funding to purchase it.
3 Rent out the property.
4 Periodically, review the property's value and the income it generates. Decide whether to carry on renting or sell at a profit.

But what if you have the money in your bank account? You don't need to borrow to buy a property or invest in a business, so why is it a good idea to borrow? These are good questions. Many of us have been told, or we feel intuitively, that getting into debt is a bad thing. Sometimes it's necessary, but if you can afford to purchase something outright, that is surely the preferred option.

Well, I would invite you to observe the example set by Facebook founder, Mark Zuckerberg. Despite being one of the world's richest men, he doesn't own his house outright. Like many of us, he has a mortgage. Now we can safely assume that, regardless of the size of the property, paying cash would have been well within his reach. Instead, he chooses to make monthly payments to his lender of choice. Surely that's a burden he could rid himself of. Famously, Beyoncé and Jay-Z also have a mortgage.

But using borrowed money is part of the billionaire mindset. Mark Zuckerberg chooses to pay a mortgage to maintain cashflow as opposed to depleting cash reserves by making a one-off purchase. We have made a similar decision. Our house still has a mortgage. We could clear that debt but it makes sense to repay a manageable sum every month while having money available for other purposes.

At one level this is a decision just about anyone might make. For instance, if £1,000 is owed on a credit card there's a spectrum of choice between paying the whole debt in one fell swoop or scheduling repayments in increments. The staggered approach will be more expensive in terms of interest but it means the borrower has £1,000 in ready cash, with the monthly credit card bill being paid as new income comes in. The choice is really down to the individual. If debt isn't really a problem, rushing to pay off loans can limit your options. There is, therefore, an opportunity cost.

Leverage can be tax efficient. In the USA in particular, billionaires tend to pay little or no money to the tax authorities because of the way their affairs are structured. As highlighted by wealth management company BNY Mellon, the net worth of millionaires and billionaires tends to be mostly derived from investments in assets. There is no tax to pay on such assets – such as shares or property – until a sale is made. Then capital gains tax falls due. To avoid this, the wealthy borrow against the value of their portfolios to free up living expenses and also make new investments. In this way, tax is mitigated.

The truth is that the very rich tend to borrow a lot more money than those who are not well off. They are comfortable with debt because they know they can use leverage to make money tax efficiently. To take just one example, an individual with a portfolio of shares and other assets might need cash to finance his or her lifestyle or other activities. Selling assets to raise cash would trigger a tax charge. By borrowing against the portfolio, the tax event is avoided. To some extent, anyone with a major asset – such as a property – can do something similar by borrowing against the equity to cover big expenses.

Seen from that perspective, debt is a tool. Using credit strategically and sensibly can help grow your wealth and make money. It's not something to be afraid of. But recognize bad debt when you see it and take action to clear it.

The Rich Forever checklist

- Understand the difference between good and bad debt.
- Audit your finances and identify bad debt.
- List your current good and bad debt.
- If you have a debt problem, acknowledge it.
- Make a plan to clear your debt. That may involve paying more every month.
- Link that plan to a budget. Look at the money coming and going out. Take steps to either increase your income or reduce outgoings (you can do both). This in turn frees cash to repay debts more quickly.
- Use debt for positive purposes. Borrow to pay for things that will enhance your life in the longer term. List three things that will positively enhance your life in the long term by using debt.
- Consider leverage – using borrowed money to pay for assets that in turn generate an income higher than the debt repayments. What opportunities are available to leverage debt currently?

CHAPTER FIVE

Money Management Made Easy – Saving and Budgeting

Renowned motivational speaker Tony Robbins shared a social post that stated 'You either master money or, on some level, money masters you' which is why this book is dedicated to money mastery. One unexpected by-product of the COVID pandemic was an increase in personal savings. In retrospect that's not surprising. As the US Federal Reserve noted in 2022, state transfers of money to individuals aimed at cushioning the impact of restrictions actually boosted household budgets at a time when people had less to spend their money on.

The UK saw a similar trend. A report by Bowmore Financial Planning suggested savings increased by 3.93 per cent in the year to November 2022. As in the USA, people who saved during the pandemic have continued to do so. It became a habit.

Now, having money to save or invest is undoubtedly a good thing. For one thing, a surplus of cash in your bank account suggests that more money is coming in than going out every month. That fact alone can do wonders for your sense of security.

But is saving a virtue in itself? Well, yes – but only up to a point. But if you're lucky or diligent enough to be saving regularly, you should probably be asking yourself a few questions.

First and foremost, what are your reasons for saving? Are you saving to ensure there's something left in the financial tank if your income falls? Or have you something specific in mind, such as the deposit on a house, a new car or a designer jacket?

Are you, perhaps, saving for saving's sake, with no real reason other than the satisfaction of putting money in the bank? If that's the case, is that arrangement working for you?

Why you need a plan

There's nothing wrong with any of the above motives. But simply putting a portion of your income into a bank savings account every month won't necessarily help you achieve your long-term financial goals. As with so many things in life, it is much better to have a plan that addresses your needs in the short, medium and longer term.

The plus side of saving is that it does create a pot of money that is available when required. The cash is there when the time comes to buy a house. Or, if you're planning a dream holiday, you won't have to max out on the credit card to pay for it, because you've diligently saved.

But I would suggest you ask yourself *how much* you need to save? The annual interest paid on savings accounts is often lower than the inflation rate, meaning that any money kept in a bank account will lose value. That was particularly true in the wake of the pandemic and at the onset of the war in Ukraine. Annual inflation – the percentage rise in prices over a year – spiralled higher in most countries while returns on savings remained stubbornly low. Central bank interest rates have risen from all-time lows, but savings rates rarely go up by the same amount.

In the UK, even high-interest accounts – which usually have restrictions around accessing the cash – were posting interest rates of 5.0 per cent when we were writing this book (early 2023). Set against retail price inflation of more than 10 per cent, that wasn't good. In the USA, inflation climbed to 9 per cent before falling back after the start of the war in Ukraine. The best savings rates were around 4.2 per cent. These were extreme times, but even if central banks achieve an on-target inflation rate of 2.00–2.5 per cent, money held in a bank will not deliver huge returns and its value may continue to erode.

Again, I would stress that saving is a good thing. All you really need to look at is how much you need sitting in the bank. After all, there are many other things you could be doing with your money.

But that begs another question. How can you possibly know how much you're going to need to have in the bank in five, ten or fifteen years' time? Well, you can budget for the near, medium and long term. And once you've done that, you can create a savings and investment strategy.

Money for emergencies

There are some things you should be planning for right away, namely those life-changing events and emergencies that cause real problems unless there is cash available to deal with them.

For instance, It's a good idea to have an emergency budget that will enable you to survive should life take a 180-degree turn.

You could think of this as 'f**k you money'. There are times when you need to get out of a situation. A bad relationship, perhaps, or a toxic work environment. Now, one of the reasons people hang around longer than they should in certain circumstances is a lack of money. It might feel great to leave a job, but not if the alternative is an enormous financial black hole. Equally, leaving a relationship can have severe financial implications, especially if it means walking out of a shared home.

Having a savings pot enables you to take control of your own destiny. You could also think of it as 'vex' money. My mother used to advise that, when going out on a date, I should always have the appropriate funds to pay for my meal and travel home in case things went wrong. This is true of dating as it is true of life. If something is vexing you, do you have your financial situation organized in such a way so as to give you an easy exit?

Personal survival costs

Closely related to this is personal survival money. You can characterize this as the percentage of income you set aside either to get you through difficult times or to help you take advantage of opportunities that arise.

For instance, if you lose your job, you'll need money to survive until another employer is found. That could be days, weeks or months, and during that period the bills won't stop piling up below the letterbox.

More positively, you might want to start a business. That will require enough money to live on until the revenues begin to flow in. Every business is different. Sometimes you collect the money as soon as a product or service is delivered to the customer, so cash begins to come in relatively quickly. Often, though, a customer will be invoiced and might take a month (or if your client is a corporate brand it could be as long as 3 months) to pay, so there are delays (if your client is a corporate brand, the wait time could be as long as three months). Typically, it will take months or years to build a customer base. It's difficult to start a business without a float of cash. The necessary funding can be borrowed, of course, but you'll be in a much stronger position – or at the very least have a wider range of options – if there is money to live on when it's needed.

It's important to remember that emergency and personal survival savings pots are not nest eggs. Their purpose is not necessarily to provide you with the cash for a comfortable retirement or the wherewithal to help your children through university or to assist them in purchasing their first houses. This is money to help you deal with some of the tough choices and circumstances inevitably thrown up by life.

It is practical money. and if it is to serve its purpose, there needs to be enough of it. I would recommend planning to have enough money to survive reasonably comfortably for three or six months.

So how much do you need?

If you ask that question out of the blue to just about anyone, the truth is they probably would quote a figure based on a rough idea of their monthly spend. The figure could well be wrong. By the time we hit a certain age, our bank accounts are peppered with direct debits paying for mortgages, telecom costs, utilities, insurance, subscriptions, charitable donations, family commitments and a host of other things. Some of them – such as utility bills and rental or mortgage costs – will spring easily to mind. Others – even the essentials – get forgotten.

To work out how much you need to save for emergencies, it's important to have all the figures at hand – not only the direct debits but also the costs associated with putting petrol in the car, travelling to work or going to the supermarket. Happily, a quick check through the monthly outgoings of your main bank account – and also credit card spending – provide the numbers. Some of the spending will be essential, but not all of it.

Using either a spreadsheet or pen and paper, you can begin to work out exactly what's required to cope with an emergency situation over a period of months.

Work out:

- overall expenditure
- your financial health (debts etc.)
- basic outgoings
- non-essentials aka 'fun money'.

This will give you the big picture. Once you've done that, you can begin to hone a survival plan. For instance, you could decide what direct debits you have to maintain in certain situations and those that can be exited. Mobile phone, yes; multiple streaming subscriptions, maybe not so much. It's about personal choices.

This is also a great opportunity to identify potential savings. As contracts come to an end, they can often be renegotiated or switched. For instance, a quick trawl of comparison sites could pull up better insurance deals. When a mobile phone contract comes to an end, the option is there to switch to calls and data only, rather than upgrading to a payment plan for a new handset. In other words, are there ways to reduce outgoings without any impact on your standard of life?

You may even discover direct debits you don't need, even when budgeting isn't an issue.

And here's the magic. You may never need to tap into your emergency and personal survival savings but mapping out a budget provides a golden opportunity to really get on top of your financial affairs and perhaps also have an honest internal conversation about what has been going right, what's been going wrong, and what might be improved.

The ideal way to do this is to use a budget tracker, a tool that will help you make sense of your finances on an ongoing basis. This is what a budget tracker might look like. We've allocated a page to aspects of your finance such as income, savings, expenses and debt.

Rich Forever Monthly Smart Money Tracker

Date	Income Source	Goal	Actual
	Salary		
	Business Income / Dividends		
	Income from Investments e.g. Property		
	Unexpected Income		
Income Total			

Savings	Goal	Actual
Cash Account		
Investment Account		
Emergency Fund		
Retirement Fund		
Holiday Fund		
Total		

Fixed Expenses	Goal	Actual
Mortgage		
Phone Bill		
Internet		
Subscriptions		
Insurance (life, home, car, medical)		
Total		

Fixed Variable Expenses	Goal	Actual
Food		
Transport		
Clothing		
Household Bills		
Family (childcare or other)		
Total		

Unexpected Expenses	Goal	Actual
Car Fines		
Prescriptions		
Emergency Health		
Household		
Family		
Total		

Luxury Expenses	Goal	Actual
Dining Out		
Gym		
Hair & Beauty		
Entertainment		
Personal Development		
Subscriptions (non essential)		
Home Delivery		
Total		

Debt	Goal	Actual
Car Loan		
Credit Card 1		
Credit Card 2		
Personal Loan 1		
Other		
Total		

Budget Summary	Goal	Actual
Income Total		
Fixed Total		
Fixed Variable Total		
Luxury Expenses Total		
Savings Total		
Debt Total		
Unexpected Expenses Total		
Total		

Making sacrifices

You should also think about saving for the things that bring joy into your life. Material things are not superficial. They make us feel better about ourselves. Some are cheap, but others require a much bigger outlay – these are the items you save for.

You can see this in terms of sacrifice or deferred gratification. You are reducing your disposable income today in order to have the funds available for something beneficial in the longer term.

We live in a world in which both gratification and credit are instant. Credit cards, store cards, instant borrowing at website shopping carts and bank loans are all easily available. We don't have to wait for the things we want to buy. We can simply purchase today and repay the debt at leisure.

There are times when it makes sense to borrow. Equally though, debts can mount up over time, making life much more difficult than it needs to be for our future selves.

Saving for specific items has a number of advantages. First and foremost, when it's bought, it's paid for. But saving also provides a degree of perspective. The item you acquire won't be an impulse purchase. Instead, it will be something you've thought about and worked hard for. As such, deferring gratification can add a degree of pride to the purchase.

If you are saving for something major – a really nice car would be a case in point – it helps to motivate yourself. For instance, visualize it. Imagine how it will feel to drive. Perhaps call around to the local dealership to take one out for a spin.

Savings goals change. If we stick with that car, for example, it may be that once you've saved the necessary sum, the shine begins to wear off a little. Maybe that money could be spent on something else. Travel perhaps. The truth is that priorities change. There are things we think we want but, when the cash is available, it turns out they aren't so important after all. You're over it. But that's OK. If you decide you'd like to take six months off to travel rather than buy a new car, the money is there.

It is worth spending a little time thinking about what your saving priorities are. If you have your heart set on a certain item, is it what you really want? What part will it play in your quality of life? What gap will it fill? Would the money be better spent on something else?

This is where it can get tricky. Most people don't have unlimited resources. Targeting a particular object of desire can provide a motivation to save but it can also confuse matters. Maybe, you aspire to wear a £10,000 watch. You've saved for it. You can afford it. But you also want a long-haul holiday that costs about the same. Suddenly, you have choices and the decision isn't so clear-cut.

My advice would be to make your choices carefully. A simple exercise can assist decision making. Rate the items from one to ten according to how they will affect your life. Will it make you happier? Will it improve your health? Will it provide you with more confidence? Will it help to enhance your network or opportunities?

Now, if choosing proves impossible, you might just decide that the money would be better left in your bank account. Fair enough, but that's a choice as well. Would you rather have the cash or that Rolex watch? That's up to you, but it's important to remember that spending is an important part of life. There are all sorts of good reasons to save and invest, but remember to have fun. Enjoy the money you've worked for.

We all need the gratification that comes from going to the shops and buying something that enhances our lives or is simply fun to own. But there's a validation factor, too. The fact that we can go out and spend, reminds us we are doing OK. The life path we've chosen is delivering rewards. For some, those rewards might be experiences.

Really it's a case of budgeting holistically, taking into account the money saved for emergencies, personal survival and the goals you've set yourself. Factored into that is the money you need for everyday life – the fun stuff, such as going out, buying clothes, helping others, charitable giving and all the essentials. When you think of your life in the round, you can then begin to allocate parts of your monthly income.

Set aside a percentage for saving. Maybe you can afford to set aside a third of your salary. After a while, when you have enough in the bank to feel secure, the next step is to allocate money to investments that can deliver a higher return.

So let's say you've been saving for a while. You have enough money to deal with emergencies. You can then put 40 per cent of your savings allocation into higher-return investments. That could be a relatively safe investment that will nonetheless see your money working harder – a stocks and shares fund tracking a major index such as the FTSE 100 or an index provider like the S&P would be a case in point. All investments carry an element of risk but that's OK, because you also have money in the bank as a security blanket. You can have a pot of safe money. another for moderate risk and perhaps a third for higher-return, higher-risk investments.

A budget for life

We all aspire to live in a way that satisfies us, and money is a key component in helping is to do just that. In order to achieve our life goals, it's important that we look at the money that's going to be required to sustain our chosen lifestyles up until retirement and beyond. Again, we need to budget.

The truth is there are a lot of demands on our wallets and bank accounts. We want good food, entertainment, holidays, cars and houses. We think it's a good idea to invest in stocks and shares. Again, more cash. Going to university seems like a good long-term investment but it requires money that could be spent on other things. Children arrive. Parents get old. Life gets complicated and so do our financial affairs.

So just as you allocate funds for saving and investment, it also makes sense to budget for all aspects of your life, from everyday spending to long-term goals.

A good place to start is by taking a step back. What does your life look like? What are you setting out to achieve? And how will you finance it? It's helpful to divide things up into segments and assign budgets and targets accordingly. You should consider:

- **Lifestyle** This category would include the home you want to live in, travel plans and material objects. How much will they cost and how will they be paid for?
- **Personal development** This is something that can all too easily be forgotten. The truth is we don't enter into adulthood fully formed. To succeed, we need skills,

information and education. That principle applies to our careers, business activities, and serious interests and hobbies. Without the life skills and appropriate knowledge, you won't get far. It's the same with activities such as investment. Few people succeed as investors — whether it's in shares, bonds, art or property — without taking time to learn about the market. Some of the information required will be free but certainly not all of it. So assign a budget for education, mentoring and coaching when required.

- **Children** When you're relatively young, you might not spend too much time thinking about the financial commitments associated with family. You've gone out into the world to make your way. It's not always the case, but very often parents are content to look after themselves while perhaps helping you out at times. Further down the line, however, there may well be children to think of. Planning for their legacy becomes imperative. In addition to feeding and clothing them, you may wish to think about including a budget for:
  - private school fees, if appropriate
  - a contribution to university fees and living costs
  - helping them onto the property ladder — your children may need your help to find the deposits on their first homes.
- **Family support** Inevitably your parents grow older and they may need assistance with care needs and so on.
- **Investing** If you want to see the value of your money increase, while also establishing additional streams of income other than salary, then investment should be an essential component of your budgeting.

Setting goals

Now that's a big menu. It's also a list without numbers attached. Lifestyle, home, children, parents, investment. Those are things that most of us will have to finance at some time in our lives, and we should be budgeting for them as soon as possible.

But there's no real clarity here. How much does it cost to fund our travel and lifestyle aspirations? Everyone will have a different view on that. What kind of budget do we need to set aside for educating and helping our children and parents? Again, there is no one-size-fits-all answer.

Faced with a spinning black hole of options, it is all too easy to not do any planning at all. Yes, there may be some things you need to save for in the years ahead, but exactly what that will mean in cash terms is hard to predict. But no matter, there is plenty of time. Something will turn up. It's a comforting thought.

Of course, sometimes things do turn up. A legacy. A lottery win. Business success. A rapid rise in salary as promotion follows promotion. But, in reality, the best way to ensure you have the money you need is to set yourself financial goals and a strategy to achieve them. Once you know what you need, you can work towards achieving your ambitions.

Your goals should be clear and measurable. A fuzzy, ill-defined objective won't be of much use to you. Byron and I are big fans of goal setting so much so that in a previous book, *The Business Survival Kit*, we devoted a whole chapter to it. Why? Because your goals should be so clear that you could send it to a factory to manufacture. Yet so many people go about life *thinking* they have clear goals, when really all they have is a list of dreams.

Think of it this way. How many times have you heard someone commit themselves to 'getting fitter'? It's a resolution that is usually made in and around the New Year or after a particularly unsettling encounter with the bathroom scales.

That's great. No one would argue that getting fitter is anything but a good thing. But the resolution probably won't bear fruit unless the outcome is clarified. Getting fitter could mean gentle exercise that results in some welcome but relatively minor improvements to heart strength and lung capacity. Or it could mean training to run a marathon within 12 months.

The clearer the goal, the more likely it is to succeed. Someone training for a 42k run knows the objective and can create an appropriate training programme that will itself have sub-goals. Being able to run 5k in a month, 10k in six months, followed by a half marathon.

Importantly, the would-be marathon runner will be able to use these milestones on the road to track their progress.

Someone who simply wants to get fitter, on the other hand, won't have any benchmarks or targets. In the absence of anything to measure progress, the good intentions of the first few weeks of running or going to the gym could evaporate over the following months. The couch begins to look considerably more tempting.

You can apply the same principle to budgeting and planning. Simply saying, 'I would like to be a homeowner', isn't really a goal as such. It's a fuzzy aspiration. It becomes a goal when the objective begins to firm up: what's the location? The type of apartment or house? The cost? The timescale for the purchase?

That kind of ambition probably sits alongside other lifestyle ambitions. The desire to travel. To eat in good restaurants. Or to wear nice clothes. In fact, there's probably going to be a considerable amount of overlap. Few people aspire simply to acquire their dream home. It's only one part of the jigsaw.

And that's where you hit the challenges. How do you balance your priorities and achieve all those life goals while also having money for some of the things that perhaps sit just on the other side of the horizon, such as bringing up children and saving for retirement.

An effective and realistic plan

A good place to start is to work out – as best you can – how much you need. Byron, as we saw in Chapter 1, calls this 'knowing your number'. Look five, ten, twenty, thirty years ahead. Decide where you want to be financially, tot up the component costs and arrive at a number.

Once a figure has been arrived at, you can begin to look at how you will get to where you want to be. How much money is required? What annual income is needed to support the goals you've set down? And where will that income come from? Salary? Running a business? Savings? Investments?

The next stage is to plot the execution. In other words, your plan to earn, save, invest and develop appropriate income streams. This part of the plan should have a timeline in the form of targets with dates attached. Buying a four- or five-bedroom house – if that's the plan – shouldn't be an abstract concept; it should be something you aim to acquire within an achievable timeframe. You can do this with all your financial goals. Six months to save for a car. A year or two to build a pot of emergency savings. Over a longer period, you might aim for a £100,000 nest egg.

It's important to set realistic deadlines. Little can be gained from aiming for something that is not clearly defined or out of practical reach. That said, it might be absolutely possible to achieve at least some of your goals more rapidly than you imagine. In his book *The 12 Week Year*, productivity expert Brian Moran argues that setting long timelines can be counterproductive.

For instance, if you're in business, you might set a target to triple sales over 12 months. On a personal level, that would certainly boost your income and capacity to save. But, as Moran points out, a lot can happen over a year. The business could start well with its sales drive and then run out of steam. The alternative is to set shorter timescales for your goals and work to realize them as rapidly as possible. Twelve-week targets instil a much needed sense of urgency, he says.

You can apply a similar principle to a whole range of targets. Clear debts sooner rather than later. Or create that emergency pot in six months. Again, you'll need a plan to help you achieve faster. That could be as simple as channelling a higher percentage of income into savings for a limited period. Or if the target is a £100,000 nest egg, the execution might involve the acquisition and sale of investment properties, using rental to pay off a buy-to-let mortgage while the value of the asset appreciates ahead of selling and reaping the profit.

The key to effective goal setting is to put it all down in black and white. You can do this on a spreadsheet, but, in the first instance at least, it's helpful to buy a large-format notepad or loose-leaf pages and write down all your goals, along with your plans to achieve them.

You might also find it helpful to do a deal with yourself. If the target is to have £50,000 in the bank in five years, write a cheque to yourself for that amount, place it in an envelope with a date on the front and put it in a drawer, wallet or purse. It will act not only as a reminder of the target but also as a means to visualize what you're seeking to achieve. This gives the objective — which may be some way down the line — a kind of tangible reality in your mind.

Equally, if your goal is to invest in property. Visit as many houses and apartments as possible. Whet your appetite as a potential owner. Visualize your goals.

Don't expect any of this to be set in stone. As you go through life, priorities will change and, with them, ambitions. Don't be afraid to reassess your life goals and plan accordingly.

And start with what is possible. Initially focus on the basics. Target income, accommodation, a decent lifestyle and enough savings to give you a degree of security. After that, you might choose to invest more. But always do what's right for you in terms of delivering the life you aspire to. Identify goals, set budgets and execute a plan.

The Rich Forever checklist

- Are you saving? If so, ask yourself what you are saving for.
- Plan for emergencies. Set a goal to save money equivalent to three to six months' living costs to cover you should you lose your income or need to step away from a difficult situation such as a toxic working environment or a failed relationship.
- Work out how much you will need for that period (bills, housing costs, etc.).
- Set priorities for the things you might want to, or need to, save for — holidays, children and university costs are just a few examples.
- Set a savings goal.
- Plan the execution of that goal.
- Save a percentage of your income in alignment with the goal.

CHAPTER SIX
The Truth about Stocks and Shares

In an address to students in New York City, Warren Buffet said 'Risk comes from not knowing what you're doing' but that does not have to be your reality. To many people, the word 'investment' is synonymous with buying shares. That's partly down to the attention paid to the world's stock markets by newspapers and television. The ever-shifting fortunes of the world's share markets are often seen as a bellwether of economic wellbeing. So whenever inflation soars and interest rates move up or down to fight it, or the latest growth figures point to boom or recession, finance journalists are usually quick to analyse the impact on stocks and shares.

In that sense, we are all aware of the importance of shares. At the same time, we've probably also heard no end of stories about those who have made 'a killing' buying and selling shares – not just the professionals who work on the trading floors or financial centres but also those who actively invest from the comfort of their own homes using their laptops, tablets and phones. On the other side of the coin, there are also plenty of examples of people who have played the market and lost all or a proportion of their life savings.

There are ways and means to benefit from the stock markets without really thinking about it. If you contribute to a pension fund, a significant percentage of your money will be invested in shares by the pension fund managers. The same is true if you put money into a shares-based managed fund. In these cases, you are not personally picking stocks. Instead, you are benefitting from the expert choices made by third parties. When you invest in a fund, your money is pooled with the contributions of other investors. The fund manager then uses the pot of cash to buy assets.

Funds of this type are a relatively safe option when viewed over the medium and long term, particularly if they concentrate on shares within a major index such as the FTSE 100 or S&P 500.

These 'indices' are essentially groupings of companies. For instance, the FTSE 100 is made up of the top companies in the UK according to their valuation. When the FTSE goes up or down by, say, 5 per cent, that figure is really an average of how companies within the index have moved. They provide a useful guide to the state of the markets.

The major indices are comprised of well-established companies. The value of their shares – when averaged out – probably won't grow that rapidly, but they represent a stable proposition that should deliver a better return than money placed in a bank account. There are also funds offering higher returns. This is usually based on investment in companies with growth potential. As ever, the higher the possible return, the greater the risk.

Increasingly, however, many of us are choosing to make our own investment decisions, using online services. Trading apps allow us to pick stocks, purchase them and then – if things go according to plan – sell at a profit when their value rises.

There's no right and wrong. Depending on who you are, and what you're setting out to achieve, investing via a pension scheme, a managed fund, directly through an app or a combination of all three could represent the best approach. But whatever way you choose to invest, it's important to understand the market and devise a strategy that will deliver serious returns.

What are stocks and shares?

But what exactly are we talking about here? First of all, let's have a look at the terminology. The phrase 'stocks and shares' is a little confusing. Aren't they, you might ask, more or less the same thing?

Almost, but not quite. A company's stock is essentially the sum of its shares. If you buy shares in a company – whether 100 or 1,000 – you are buying stock. A share, on the other hand, is the smallest unit of ownership.

Shares deliver a return to investors in two ways. First, if a company is making a profit it will usually pay a dividend to its shareholders to keep them on board. So, if you're an investor, a payment will be made at regular intervals. Just how big that payment will be depends on two things: the number of shares in your possession; and the dividend per share set by the company.

The expected dividend is often at the heart of the case for buying stock in a well-established business. Their share prices don't move that much, but they attract shareholders because consistent profits feed through to an ability (usually) to pay dividends.

Second – and this is the focus for a lot of active investors – if the value of a share rises, then you can sell at a profit.

That's if you own the shares directly. If you invest through a fund that pools the cash of many investors, then it will mediate the payment of dividends and the profits from trading. This is because managed funds – for example unit trusts – invest in shares on behalf of clients who do not themselves own the stock directly. When the companies in the portfolio pay dividends, these go to the fund rather than individual investors. The fund then manages the payment of returns.

The price of shares goes up and down for all sorts of reasons, but at root it's a question of supply and demand. If more people want to buy into a certain company, the value of its stock will rise.

The history of stock markets

Stock trading in its modern form is generally agreed to have kicked off in the early 17th century when the Dutch East India Company needed to raise funds to finance its activities. To do that, it sold shares to the public. In return for committing their capital, investors received dividends.

In itself, that wouldn't have signalled any kind of a financial revolution. The concept of buying into a company wasn't new. But the Dutch East India also created what is known today as a market. Those who owned shares could buy more or sell their stock to others. Unlike today, however, the only shares traded were those of the East India company itself.

The idea caught on. Share trading mechanisms were created in other countries including the UK. Investors – some of them at least – enthusiastically embraced the idea of buying into potentially successful ventures.

The concept of the stock exchange began to emerge. In London, back in 1698, John Castaing created a list of company shares that could be traded at his favourite coffee house. Just over a century later, London became home to a 'regulated' exchange, the forerunner of today's London Stock Exchange.

In the USA, the Philadelphia Stock Exchange was founded in 1790 and a few years later – 1817, to be precise – the New York Stock and Exchange Board was formed.

Sadly, it wasn't all plain sailing. Fortunes were made but there were also some real financial disasters, including the infamous South Sea Bubble.

The South Sea Company was a joint venture between businessmen and the British government and was established to pay off the national debt using trading profits. It attracted huge numbers of excited investors and its share price rose to £1,000 before plunging to £124. In reality, it was a kind of Ponzi scheme, with investor cash rather than trading profits paying the government debt. But it was also a reminder that share prices can rise as well as fall. The scale of the financial disaster also led to tighter regulation to restore confidence in the market concept. So something good came out of bad.

Technology changes the game

The broad principles of share trading have remained more or less unchanged, but in terms of execution – or, to put it another way, how the trades are carried out – today's markets are almost unrecognizable from their 18th- and 19th-century forebears.

For almost three centuries, buying and selling took place in physical spaces, but in the 1970s and 1980s deregulation – known as the Big Bang in the UK – opened the door to new technology in the shape of computers and networks.

In the late 1990s, the mass rollout of the internet opened up the markets to private investors. People who would previously have had no choice but to go along to a local stockbroker to execute the buying and selling of shares could do it themselves on their own home computers. That removed a barrier. For many people, popping down to see a financial professional with instructions to buy and sell shares was just too much trouble. Added to that, the involvement of a stockbroker could make it seem that trading shares was something very much in the hands of a third party. It wasn't something that most people could experiment with themselves. The Big Bang combined with apps put power in the hands of the people.

As a result, day trading came into vogue. This was an activity that involved buying and selling a group of shares in the space of a day in order to make profits when prices went up. It was something that was – and still is – undertaken by professionals working for investment houses but also private individuals. It was probably the day trading boom of the 1990s and 2000s that really embedded the idea that active trading could be a pathway to riches.

In reality, though, banking profits often requires a longer-term approach.

Fast-forwarding to the present day, a wide range of trading apps and programmes are available. The opportunity to invest directly in shares has been opened to everyone with an internet connection.

The long term

Is this a good thing? I would say, broadly speaking, yes, absolutely. Stocks and shares represent an important asset class, and it is absolutely possible to make money, particularly when you take a longer-term approach.

But here's the caveat. Investing in shares is not a risk-free undertaking. We all know that average prices across the markets move up and down – often in response to economic news – as do individual stocks.

So, in one scenario, you might spread your risk across a number of stocks. Then along comes a bad piece of economic news and more or less everything in the market falls, as does the value of your investment. The good news is that just as markets fall, they invariably rise. Over time the value of a balanced portfolio of shares will usually continue on an upward trajectory, albeit with some dips. And one-day falls are often followed by a bounce in the other direction. That's where the longer-term perspective comes in.

Every so often, things can get scary. Economies go into recession and the world's markets lose value for protracted periods. History suggests, however, that recovery always follows sooner or later. Admittedly, that can take a while. After the great financial crash in the late 2000s, the Standard and Poor Index of 500 leading global shares lost about half its value and took almost two years to recover. But eventually it did climb back. Investing requires a certain amount of bravery and an understanding of the way markets perform over time.

Why do markets move?

Stock market crashes are unpredictable, not least because they are triggered by different kinds of events. The crash of 2000 was largely due to a loss of confidence in so-called dot-com internet companies. In 2008 it was the financial crisis. In 2020 the COVID-19 pandemic was the cause. There have been other market setbacks – small and large – over the last 20 years. Some have been short-lived, others longer lasting. There has yet to be a market 'correction' – a downward movement – without a recovery.

Movements in the share price of an individual company are a slightly different matter. Markets move because of sentiment, underpinned by economic data and conditions. Individual share prices move (mostly) because of how a company is performing and how it is perceived. Some companies are undervalued, meaning they are underappreciated and thus have the potential to gain in value.

A smart investor can buy under-priced stock in the expectation that a good company's share price will rise once other investors realize what they are missing. That enables you to bank the profits. The problem is that some shares don't rise. They fall and perhaps do not recover even if the market as a whole is on a rising tide.

Selecting individual shares is known as stock-picking. I find this a fascinating and engaging process. It's also potentially very profitable but there aren't any guarantees of success. Get the judgement call right and you make a lot of money. Get it wrong and you're out of pocket. Sometimes you might simply break even or make a decent return over months and years.

But it's not simply a case of selecting stocks. Decisions have to be made about when to buy and sell. Let's say you own shares in Apple and you see them rising. Your goal is to make profits but at what point do you sell? Do you wait for the share to rise further or decide it's hit a peak already? Again, it's about choosing the right moment. And if a share is falling, do you sell, hang on in the hope of recovery, or buy more?

All this can seem, to say the least, daunting, but it shouldn't be. With a good strategy, an investor might see a ten-times return over seven years. Not many asset classes can offer that.

Investing in shares can be tax efficient. In the UK, ISAs allow savers to put cash or shares to the value of £20,000 per year into an individual savings account, with no income or capital gains tax to be paid on the return. The ISA can wrap the investments from a managed fund or your own personal share selections. A similar scheme known as IRA (Individual Retirement Account) operates in the USA. Stocks and Shares ISAs are a good way to begin investing. At the present moment, only 3 per cent of people in the UK have a stocks and shares ISA – this is an astonishing statistic given the top 10 per cent of people in the UK earn at least £65,000.

Getting started

That's the background, but at this point, you may be asking, is investing in stocks and shares really something that anyone can do? And as a non-professional, is it possible to make money?

Well, there's a learning curve. I began to actively invest in shares during the pandemic. I signed up to a couple of trading apps – Trading 212 and Freetrade, to be precise – and began to look at the market. To be honest, I didn't necessarily have a strategy. I was looking for shares that were in demand and companies that stood a good chance of being around in 20 years' time. Using those criteria, I purchased Tesla and Greatland Gold – two very different stocks. Tesla remains the most iconic electric vehicle brand in the market. Greatland Gold is a natural resources company.

Their respective fortunes indicate that stock picking isn't an exact science. As I write this, Tesla is down around 40 per cent. Greatland Gold on the other hand is up 39 per cent. Overall my portfolio is currently down £6,000, but this is a long game and you have to have realistic expectations. Crucially, you have to remember that things can take time to play out.

And, with the right strategy, it is possible to make serious returns.

That's something that Debodun Osekita has proved after a social experiment of growing his pension portfolio (through a self-invested personal pension, or SIPP) by ten times over a period of seven years while sharing this journey with members of his now *Forbes*-featured Stock Pickers Academy (SPA) in that period.

SPA is a digital community with over 5,000 members of which 1,000 are investing professionals from his personal network. Having worked for a combined 12 years as an equities (stocks) trader at investment bank Goldman Sachs, a family investment office, Barclays and a quantitative multi-asset hedge fund (where algorithms are built to systematically invest in the global market over short-, medium- and long-term time-frames), he today works as an investing coach – a personal trainer for investing! He has a real-time watchlist of over a thousand stocks, ETFs (ready-made portfolios) and REITs (which enable you to use the stock market to invest in property), and provides advice and tuition for people who want to use the stock market as a means to beat inflation and build wealth over the longer term. He also leverages his network to help angel investors get access to shares in private companies like Revolut, Stripe, OpenSea, ChatGPT (OpenAi) and start-ups with founders from underrepresented backgrounds.

A great deal of Debodun's coaching is based on his own track record and strategy. Drawing on his background as a trader, he set himself the task of starting with a £5,000 investment – the money in that aforementioned pension pot – and growing that to provide himself £1 million on retirement. In four years, he had tripled his investment. After six to seven years the value of the pot had grown to £50,000. That kind of return rate (38 per cent average return) puts him on target to hit or exceed his initial retirement target. He usually aims for an average of 15–20 per cent each year (similar to doubling his investment after every four to five years).

There is potentially a snowball effect. If – as Debodun did – you can double the value of an investment over four years, that generates more money to invest, increasing the momentum for growth.

So the question is: how do you get started? Debodun and many others provide evidence that investing in shares can be lucrative. But how do you actually make it work for you?

Education and training

'Investing is not a game where the person with the highest
IQ makes the most money.'

Warren Buffett

Debodun believes that investing is for everyone. Long-term investing to build wealth via stocks is like learning first aid, whereas day trading to make a monthly income is like trying to become a brain surgeon. It most certainly is not for everyone. His advice to anyone considering investing in stocks and shares is to do the groundwork. 'Get a good education,' he says. 'Otherwise you won't have repeated success.'

These days, there is a huge amount of educational material and content available. There are, for example, a great many books on the subject, and if you can't find them locally, most of the major titles will be available online. You can sign up to online or offline classes or tutorial sessions. Some of the educational material is free. Some of it is paid for. There are market 'gurus' who you can follow online on platforms like YouTube but you have to be careful to check their background, track record and experience.

And there are many potential pitfalls. For instance, an online guru may be giving you what is essentially good but incomplete information. You don't see the big picture and, therefore, struggle with the practical application.

Now, pulling together information and using it to underpin a trading strategy isn't easy. That's where a coach comes in. A good coach has read the books and has the experience but more importantly can teach in a language you can understand and feel confident about. Imposter syndrome is very real when it comes to investing.

I would suggest doing a bit of homework to find a class or tutor who can give you a good grounding in the market. In practice, that means checking out their track record and reputation. A good place to start is their profile on LinkedIn.

Daunting as it seems, there's also a lot of research material: charts that can provide clues to market trends; reports on the performance of individual companies; market histories.

There is also hands-on help available to guide you as you invest. For instance, those who sign up for Debodun's SPA have access to material on investment philosophy, mindset and strategy plus a watchlist of shares that will potentially deliver good returns. In addition, members can interact with experienced investors, giving members support and access to information as they make their own choices. There are many such communities, some of them accessible through trading apps.

Community can be a hugely important factor in success. Debodun even describes investing as a 'team sport'.

That can mean a number of things. You can, for example, discuss your investment plans with others. If you see a stock that looks interesting, run it past others in the group for their opinion. They may know things that you don't.

All good teams have coaches. These are the experienced investors who are ready to spend time helping others develop investment strategies with the best chance of delivering products.

The concept of the team or community is now embedded in online share trading through the concept of copy trading. Essentially, this involves shadowing the investment decisions of others. The ability to copy trade may be offered when you sign up to a share dealing service.

It's important to pick your tribe. A community intent on fast results from day trading won't be the ideal place for an investor whose strategy is to bank gains over the long term. You may want to read that last sentence again.

Saving money

Investing in shares requires a pot of money. Now, unlike money in a bank savings account, this could be tied up in the markets and not necessarily accessible if needed for other things, so really it has to be a sum set aside for the purpose. Ideally, it should also be money that you're prepared to take a risk with. If you begin to make profits, you can of course take money out and put it in a different pot – say a college fee fund for your children – but that's a little further down the line. There are periods in life when saving is tough

Debodun's advice is to 'save when you can, over-save when you can, and when life is tough it is OK to have periods where you don't save'.

However, if you don't have money available at this very moment, a good idea is to save a proportion of your income every month with a percentage of that allocated for investment. You can treat this like a bill. Just set up a direct debit that channels a sum – it could be as little as 50 pounds or dollars – into a savings account every month. This £50 would provide a float of £600 after a year.

Once you have the necessary cash available, there are choices. For decent long-term gains, a managed fund is not a bad option. For instance, the S&P 500 global index has delivered a compound average annual growth rate of 10.7 per cent over the past 30 years.

Now during that period, there have been good years but also bad ones when the value of the S&P's basket of shares grew by very little and in some cases dropped back. But for those prepared to be long-term investors, the trajectory has been upward. So that could be a good start.

So, moving forward, maybe you'll have some money in the bank and an investment in an index-tracking fund. From that base of financial security, the next logical step is to allocate money from your investment budget for what Debodun describes as the 'riskier' stuff.

That doesn't have to be stocks and shares. For instance, Debodun's background has seen him invest in a diverse range of asset classes, both as a private individual and as a professional working for institutions. The other asset classes open to investors include cryptocurrencies, currencies (taking advantage of fluctuating exchange rates), bonds, angel investing in start-ups, commodities (oil, gold, cocoa) and property. In Debodun's view, you need to have an open mind and be prepared to try new things.

Debodun made more money in nine months from crypto than he did in his total stocks investing journey. Bear in mind, though, that crypto has its own set of risks, which we cover in Chapter 9.

It's not always necessary to buy some of these alternative assets directly. Exposure – an investor's term for possessing an investment in a particular type of asset – can be gained by buying into exchange traded funds. These are essentially vehicles using pooled money to invest in assets such as property or commodities. These funds can themselves be traded on stock exchanges.

Slow and quick money

But let's get back to shares. The companies that populate the world's major indices tend to be long-established and perhaps unexciting – banks, oil companies, retail groups and food producers. Their shares do move up and down in response to major world events such as the 2008 financial crisis or – in the case of energy companies – the war in Ukraine. But for the most part the returns across a particular index – when averaged across a balanced selection of companies – are solid but unexciting.

So if you invest in an index tracking fund, what you tend to get is slow money: steady – and actually pretty good – returns that can be relied on over a period of time with just a few hiccups. Alternatively, you could invest directly in individual companies within, say, the FTSE 100 and you might not see much movement at all.

Things become more exciting once an investor begins to pick stocks with growth potential. Now that could mean a bet on a high-profile name such as Google or Tesla – for example, buying cheap when a bit of bad news hits the stock price in the hope and belief that the value will recover before too long.

Both Google and Tesla are enormously successful companies, so their shares are pretty good bets over the longer term. But they also form part of a technology sector in which shareholders have very high expectations. If a company falls short in terms of its performance – typically reported every three months – then investors often vote with their feet and sell. Consequently, the stock falls and there are opportunities to buy more cheaply. You see this happening quite a lot in the tech sector. Google's advertising revenues come in lower than expected so its shares take a dip. Apple doesn't sell quite as many iPhones as analysts were predicting and, again, there's a decline. It can even happen if a CEO is deemed to have done something that could hit the value of the company. An example would be a sell-off of Tesla shares when Elon Musk announced plans to buy Twitter. Shareholders in the car company thought Twitter would be a distraction, so confidence in Tesla drained away. Tesla, however, is still selling a lot of cars.

Volatility and rapid market moves are not limited to the tech sector. For instance, news of a takeover bid between two publicly listed companies could send shares in the target company soaring. Equally, if the markets don't like the logic behind the proposed deal, the company planning to make the acquisition could see shareholders heading for the exit door. This provides an opportunity to buy into the target – assuming you can get there on time before the shares become unaffordable – or the acquirer if its stock tumbles and therefore seems like a bargain.

Another thing to look out for is a rights issue announcement. These are special events in which companies seeking additional finance give their existing shareholders the opportunity to buy more shares, usually at a discounted rate. Shareholders can transfer the rights to buy their stock to third parties. Potentially, there are bargains to be had for those who keep their eyes on the news.

'Stocks in the FTSE 100 don't tend to move much,' says Debodun, but there are opportunities if you look out for them.

At the other end of the spectrum, there are so-called penny stocks. These are shares in small – potentially fast-growth companies – that can be bought for around $5 or so. So if you make the right call, it's possible to make a lot of money by getting in early.

The bigger point here is that keeping a weather eye on the financial pages is an important aspect of active stock picking. It's a way of keeping up with activity in the market and also monitoring individual businesses. That means understanding the brand (and its relationship with customers) and the CEO.

There are plenty of options, including a wide range of free apps, communities and investor websites.

An investing strategy

Whether you decide to focus on large corporations, mid-sized businesses or lowly priced up-and-comers, it's important to understand the companies themselves and the factors that move their value in the marketplace. Or, to put it another way, you need to know the fundamentals of how to invest successfully. Stock picking is not easy but, as Debodun says, 'You don't need to do a course or have any knowledge to know that Apple or Amazon are great companies but what is a good price? What is a good amount to put in? When do you sell? This is why strategy is important – it takes away emotion.' There is something called first-level thinking and second-level thinking. First-level thinking says: 'Amazon is a great company – it will only get better so buy!' Second-level thinking says: 'Amazon is a great company, but its price is significantly higher than where its fundamentals say it should be because everyone has joined in on the hype. Sell! Or wait for a better price to buy.'

Investing requires not only knowledge and skills but also a workable strategy that will deliver results over time. Debodun's advice is to think long-term. 'People come to me and tell me they want to learn to trade,' he says. 'I tell them that I teach long-term investment but sometimes long-term investments can yield very short-term results due to market volatility, in which case if Christmas does come early you eat that turkey.'

Knowing when to sell or rebalance a portfolio is very important.

On the face of it, that might be at odds with the idea that stock markets can deliver a rapid rags-to-riches story. You start with a few hundred – or perhaps more realistically – a few thousand pounds or dollars – and after a period of intensive and active trading the initial investment multiplies.

Although fortunes are indeed won – and sometimes lost – you can see the stock markets as a long game. The aim is to maximize profits over years rather than days, weeks or months. That might involve periods when some of the stocks you've picked are sitting in negative territory while others are in profit. So there are decisions to be made on the best times to buy, sell or hold.

And while you are invested, there can be difficult choices and perhaps also regrets. For instance, if a stock you're holding is rising, you may sell to take profits only to see it rising further. That can be galling. It's a little bit like selling your house for a small gain over the selling price only to find that when the deal is done prices in the area have surged. Somehow you feel you have lost out, even though you are actually up on the deal.

Staying in control

A different way to look at this is to acknowledge the unpredictability of certain market movements. Stock prices fluctuate for reasons that you can't control. Yes, you can certainly exercise your best judgement. You can study the company. Look at recent movements. Take a view on whether it is over- or undervalued and make a buying or selling decision accordingly. You can also ask your community. But ultimately you can't control what happens.

But what you can do is focus on the things that can be controlled.

Debodun's view is that the ability to manage risk is crucially important. Yes, making the right stock-picking selections is vital to investment success, but so is devising a strategy that limits potential losses.

That can be as simple as limiting the amount you invest in riskier stock. If you have £1,000 to invest in shares, put some of that in a fund tracking index and use the rest – the exact proportion is up to you – for stock picking. If your choices don't come good, that's OK, because you haven't invested everything you own. If, however, they make a profit, you can take out some cash in profits and reinvest the remainder. So, you're still actively investing but not going for broke. In other words, you have a budget. I tend not to invest more than £15,000 at any one time.

Another way to hedge risk is to invest across a spread of companies. Some may gain ground and others will probably dip in value, but because you are invested in multiple stocks the chance of losing everything on just one or two stocks is greatly reduced. The same principle can be applied to investing across a range of asset classes. That's something I'll be looking at later.

With individual stocks, you can reduce risk by investing in tranches – say, initially buying £300 worth of shares and then purchasing more as you become more confident.

Now you might think the trigger for buying additional shares in a company might be a rise in the value of its shares but that's not necessarily the case.

One of Debodun's strategies is to buy into the stock at a certain price. If it falls – but he still has faith in the company – that's an opportunity to buy more. And, as he points out, the second time around you get more for your money because the shares are cheaper. This reduces the average price paid, increasing your return if and when the value of the stock rises again.

And that raises an interesting point about stock picking. In theory, you invest in good companies because their shares are going to rise. But actually your profits could be limited by the amount you've paid. Another 'not quite so good' company could well be a better bet, simply because there is a more profitable relationship between its current price and the potential of its shares to rise. The rise in its value might not be meteoric but, because you've paid a good price, your profits are ultimately bigger.

Working on the same principle, you can look for value even among world-beating or highly regarded companies. For instance, if we return to the tech sector, everyone has heard of Google and, even when its advertising revenues disappoint, you're still looking at an expensive stock. The same would apply to Apple. But the tech market is always changing. A tier or two below Google and Apple in terms of public profile, there are opportunities with businesses such as PayPal or Zoom. Now these are companies with longevity but they are also subject to price fluctuations. For instance, Zoom gained during the pandemic as demand for its video-conferencing services grew but subsequently slipped back. Depending on your viewpoint, that can be an opportunity or a cause for concern.

Value for money

'I always look at value for money,' Debodun says. 'And you can even make profits from a bad company if the price is right.'

So how does that work in practice? Well, a company can be oversold. Debodun uses the example of his decision to buy shares in GameStop, an electronics retail company that was trading at $483 before plunging to $50. 'People were shocked when I bought into it, due to the fact it was part of the meme craze and generally they know my strategies are cautious, but some of the biggest and smartest hedge funds were getting involved too,' he recalls.

His view was that the downward movement in its price had been disproportionate to the underlying of the company. Investors had overreacted. This created an opportunity. The share price fell to $30 before rising again to around $100.

That, of course, begs a question. Yes, you can make money on shares that fall out of favour, but what underpins your decision making?

Experienced traders tend to have their own systems and guidelines. For his part, Debodun has devised the concept of the 'SPA safety region'. Essentially, this is a model he has constructed.

The idea is this. The safety region is defined as the price zone that offers an opportunity to invest at a level where the probability of losing money through further price drops is kept to a minimum. The safety region model takes into a number of factors, including:

- the stock's fundamentals
- a technical analysis of the stock and its industry
- an overview of the industry (and where it is on the economic cycle)
- the company's credit rating
- the next earnings date
- the volatility of the stock (in terms of price movements)
- the company's leadership
- ratings by analysts
- recent price behaviour.

The SPA model also looks at the company's beta status, mapping how its own share performance correlates to market movements (more on that later). Sometimes, the stock won't rise by as much as expected/hoped and a quick sale could mean a small loss. Or if the stock rises above the average price you've paid, the option is there to sell at a profit quickly or wait a little longer for further gains.

You won't always get it right, but by following a strategy and allowing it to play out over time, you can rescue the risks and increase the chance of success. This is a long-term strategic approach and doesn't lend itself to an all-or-nothing, profits-today-or-bust mindset. Even day traders are playing a long game because their activity is just a snapshot of what they do over months and years.

When selecting a stock that you want to add to your portfolio, the main factors to consider are:

- the quality of the stock and its potential to gain value
- price value for money
- your own budget – how much are you prepared to pay?
- when to sell
- beta (there's an explanation of this below)
- the existing stocks in your portfolio and how any additional stock fits in with them.

You will make mistakes, and provided you manage your risk, that's not a problem because over a longer period you have an opportunity to get the majority of calls right. Debodun likes to quote the celebrated investor Warren Buffett on this point: 'Time in the market is better than timing the market.'

Diversification

One of the questions that stock pickers have to ask themselves is whether or not it's a good idea to diversify. There are various schools of thought on this.

The options are broadly this. At one end of the spectrum, you buy one or two stocks that look particularly interesting to you, and for the moment that's it. You aren't really diversifying. Your financial eggs are well and truly in one financial basket.

A second alternative is to spread the risk across a moderate number of companies. You probably wouldn't want them to look too similar in terms of their size, sector, stage of development and share price stability/volatility. The idea is, after all, to be diverse.

The volatility of a stock is – to some degree – measurable. Individual shares are given what is known as a beta rating that indicates whether they tend to move with the market, outperform or underperform. One factor when constructing a balanced portfolio is to combine stocks with different beta ratings.

Debodun is a huge advocate of beta, and yet 90 per cent of experienced retail stock investors have never heard of it, yet alone used it (you never know what you don't know until you read about it – this is why community and a coach are so important). Having a mixed-beta portfolio is important to reducing overall market risk. In simple terms, you need to know what the weather is like outside and what the season is so you dress accordingly. It might be winter but the sun might be out, so put on some shades. It might be summer but it might be forecast to rain with dark clouds looming – take an umbrella! Beta is a measure that lets you know how correlated a stock is to the overall index it is a part of. Stock picking is a micro exercise, but we live in a world driven by macro forces (economics, politics) which tend to drive broader stock market indices up and down.

Individual stocks have different sensitivities to how much they are affected and that is what beta tells you:

- **Beta can be close to 0:** if the FTSE 100 index goes up or down the stock price won't be affected much – it does its own thing regardless (e.g. Tesco).
- **Beta can be +1 or larger:** if the FTSE 100 moves up 10 per cent, it will pull the stock price up about 10 per cent; and if it goes down 10 per cent, it will drag the stock price down about 10 per cent. The larger the positive beta number is, the stronger the effect.
- **Beta can be –1 or more negative (inverse correlation):** if the FTSE 100 moves up the stock price goes down, and if it goes down the stock price moves up. The larger the negative beta number is, the stronger the effect.

The standard mathematical calculation of beta uses data over a five-year period. You can google it, but it is also on the SPA stock screener in real time.

It's also worth considering counter-cyclical stocks, which tend to do well when the economy is in a downturn.

And then if you really want to go the whole hog, you might invest across different geographies – Europe, Asia, the USA – and perhaps also multiple asset classes.

But is this a practical option?

Well, yes and no. If you have £1,000 to invest, then your scope for diversification is probably going to be limited, simply because the money you have available is going to be spread thinly over too many companies. So while there is no doubt that diversification is indeed a risk management tactic, it is not always appropriate. In that respect, an investor with £10,000 available will probably have a less diverse portfolio than someone allocating a budget of £100,000. Similarly, the £1,000,000 investor is likely to be more diverse again.

That raises the question of whether or not you need to spread the risk in any major way. Debodun thinks it is overrated as a strategy: 'In my system, someone with £5,000 might just have four stocks,' he says. 'For £100,000 that might be seven. The average person with a £10,000 investment probably has ten stocks.' You don't necessarily have to have a large and varied portfolio to do well.

Online investment platforms

A prerequisite for share trading is membership of or access to an online platform. Websites and apps have been widely available since the earliest days of the commercial internet and there are more than ever today.

The brands on offer include:

Bestinvest

Capital.com

CMC Invest

eToro

Fineco

Freetrade

Hargreaves Lansdown

IG.com

Interactive Brokers

Interactive Investor

Saxo

Trading212

Wealthify

There are in fact many more. Some are aimed at beginners; others at professionals or people with experience. There are apps that are deliberately simple to use in order to attract those in the foothills of their trading journeys. Others appear to be much more complicated, often because they are information rich. That might mean newsfeeds, charting tools, real-time quotes and copy trading or mirror trading facilities to shadow the activity of others.

Most apps will require a minimum deposit and those aimed at beginners will keep the bar quite low. It's worth checking the payment requirements (credit, debit card, etc.), the conditions around the withdrawal of money and any commissions payable on trade. Equally important, you should check the speed of execution. If you buy or sell, will that trade be actioned quickly? Some platforms allow you to invest in other assets, such as currency.

There is probably no definitive platform, but it is important to spend time researching what's on offer and finding a solution that suits your requirements.

Actively trading in the world's stock markets may turn out to be one of the most satisfying things you can do, both financially and in terms of your own personal development. It needn't be high risk if you take a measured approach.

Osekita Debodun's top tips for investment

- Invest in your education. It's vital to understand the market before you begin to invest.
- Find a coach – never ever buy anything without speaking to someone with experience. The world's greatest athletes hire coaches for a reason, and even the most talented won't be able to optimize their performance without a guiding hand. Investment is no different. Investment decisions always benefit from expert guidance. Think about how much it costs to learn to drive, buy a car through finance or cash, run a car (insurance, taxes, fuel, general maintenance) and remember that a car is a depreciating asset. You need to think about deploying similar levels of capital into owning small parts of a range of existing businesses that can increase in value (a stock portfolio!).
- When passive investing into an index fund like the S&P 500, treat each monthly payment like a bill or a mortgage payment. Pay into it consistently to reap future rewards; if you miss your monthly payment, you will regret it later!
- Investment is a team sport. Join an investing community like the free SPA telegram group and engage. Eavesdrop on discussions. This is a form of digital networking that can play a huge part in your success.
- If you buy a stock because it pays a nice dividend, it's like buying a car solely because it has a nice sound system. Dividends should be seen as a bonus rather than the main meal.
- Begin your investment journey by saving money and then allocating a portion of those savings – let's say 50 per cent – into investing then split this in two between a passive index fund strategy and an active stock picking portfolio.

- Don't worry if a share rises further after you sell. Profit is profit.
- Focus on value. You can even make money on a bad company if the price is low but has potential to rise.
- Sometimes when the price of a share falls you should buy more, as conceptually, if the stock has long-term potential and low bankruptcy risk, this means you are getting more shares for your money and a better overall average price. It's a better value proposition, though it has to be done in the right way. The SPA strategy, for example, fine-tunes these important details.
- Have a limited number of stocks in your portfolio at any given time. Someone with £5,000 might just have three stocks, each with a maximum budget which gets deployed at specific prices determined by a specific strategy like the SPA strategy.
- No matter what, don't stop!

It is worth noting that a lot of these key points have also been successfully deployed in crypto, specifically in tier one (Bitcoin, Litecoin and Ethereum).

In driving, despite passing your test you realize you have to learn the rest through experience. Investing is similar, so don't give up after a few mistakes or losses. A good coach and community help to bridge this gap. Stocks portfolios need to be monitored but strategies like the SPA's teach you how to build the right type of portfolio to match how busy you are and your lifestyle, so the amount of monitoring you need to do will match the time you realistically have available.

The Rich Forever checklist

- Save and set aside a sum of money for the purpose of trading. It should be money you can afford (and be prepared to lose) should things go wrong. Equally, you should be prepared to keep it tied up in the stock market over the long term.
- Learn as much as you can about the markets.
- Decide on a strategy – this could be aimed at a short-term gain but for most people it makes sense to take a longer-term approach. There is a spectrum running from fast to slow money.
- Find your tribe. There are many communities for traders. Join those that are aligned with your goals.
- Find a trading app that suits you. Some are feature rich but complex, while others are geared for people with less experience. Features such as communities or copy trading may be important. Ask your community questions to gain a range of answers.

CHAPTER SEVEN
Using Property to Build Wealth

Property investment is something that everyone wants to do and with good reason. Former US president Franklin D. Roosevelt said 'Real estate cannot be lost or stolen, nor can it be carried away. Purchased with common sense, paid for in full, and managed with reasonable care, it is about the safest investment in the world.' While some types of investment – such as cryptocurrency or even shares – are often perceived as slightly mysterious in terms of the forces that drive prices up and down, the property market seems to be much easier to understand. At its simplest, the value of property rests upon the fact that we all need places to live and do business. That requirement is unlikely to change any time soon, meaning that property will always have a value.

Occasionally, that value may dip or even plunge in response to rising interest rates or a recession, but, in living memory at least, the long-term trend has been upward. For instance, according to figures published by Ocean Finance, the average price of a property in the UK has risen by 78 per cent since 2000. It's a similar story in the USA. In 2000 the average home cost $200,000. Today that figure stands at more than $400,000.

Unless you are, for some reason, forced to sell during one of the market's periodic dips, the asset you purchase will rise considerably in value over time, at least if the history of the market is anything to go by.

In between buying and selling, you could be renting out your property, covering the cost of the mortgage used to buy it with a profit on top. So, you get an income combined with growth in the property's resale value.

But – and this is quite an important but – if you need a substantial amount of income, buying a property to rent to others might not give you the cashflow you need. If you're paying a mortgage on the property, that will reduce your return from the rental, as will the fees charged by managing agencies. You might find yourself making £100 a month, having spent tens or hundreds of thousands of pounds. This, of course, may vary depending on how well you buy.

So perhaps the first thing you have to remember is not to have unreasonable expectations. That's especially true if you have just one or two properties to rent.

Having said all that, property represents a great way to build long-term wealth, and actually there are quite a few options open to you. These include:

- **Buy-to-let** has been a route into the property market for countless people over the past few decades. It's a simple proposition. You buy a property – usually with a mortgage – and rent it to tenants. The property needn't be expensive, especially if you buy at an auction.
- A variation on this theme is to **buy a run-down property and refurbish it for rental**. The refurbishment means the property can command a higher rent than would otherwise have been the case. And because you've bought it relatively cheaply, the rental return – the yield – is higher. Or the property can be sold at a profit.
- **Conversions** provide another option – for instance, converting a family home into two or more apartments for sale or rental.
- **Rent-to-rent** is just what it says on the tin. You rent a property and then sublet it to tenants – assuming you have the legal right to do so. You can rent to long-term tenants or market the property as a holiday apartment or house through sites such as Airbnb.
- Ultimately, you might find yourself **investing in large-scale residential or commercial property developments**

or redevelopment projects such as building new houses or converting offices into apartments That's not something you would necessarily consider as a first- or second-time investment project but it might be something you work towards.

Getting started

But first, let's get back to basics. If you're considering a buy-to-let investment, the barrier to entry isn't high. You identify the property you want to purchase and approach a mortgage lender. Once the lender has given you a green light, you can proceed with buying the property. So, you're on your way. You can secure a buy-to-let mortgage, even if you have a relatively poor credit score. However, your rating will affect the interest rate you pay and the deposit required.

Do your homework. First and foremost, it's important to understand your own circumstances and requirements. For instance, will the property provide you with the ROI you need and does the return justify your outlay? For example, the deposit on the mortgage is an upfront cost and if that means using all your money – maybe £10,000 or £20,000 – ask yourself, is this the right investment? Does it make sense to tie that money up in property with the only return being rental income minus mortgage repayments over a period of years?

Equally, it's important to understand the market and how it works. Before you consider investing, the best thing to do is talk to as many experts as possible. The list would certainly include solicitors, mortgage advisers, estate agents and investors. If you don't have the necessary contacts, get in touch with Bianca and me. We can certainly help.

Buying a property and renting it out is a relatively simple proposition but if you're doing it for the first – or even the second or third time – you may encounter unexpected pitfalls.

If you've ever purchased a home, you'll know there's a lot that can go wrong. The seller might pull out of the deal. The survey or conveyancing process could reveal something that prompts you to withdraw your offer. The bank may decide not to give you a mortgage.

So the deal falls through and all the time you're racking up legal fees. Bear in mind the conveyancing process can take many months, so there will be a period when you are committing resources but not seeing any return in the shape of rental income.

Even after the purchase, problems can arise. You might struggle to find tenants to pay the rent you need. That shouldn't be a problem if you've researched the market. However, no landlord is immune from the problem of tenants who, for one reason or another, can't or won't pay what is owed on a regular basis. That can be a real problem if you are dependent on rental income to service your buy-to-let mortgage. This risk can now be mitigated with landlord insurance.

Real-world setbacks

Let me talk a bit about my own experience. I bought my first property at the age of 21, a two- bedroom maisonette (duplex) in the Mitcham area of South London. And, to be honest, it didn't go well. In fact, it was really stressful, not least because the tenant wasn't paying his rent. In fact, the whole thing was so stressful that I decided to sell after two years.

And you could argue that I lost out. If I had hung on to the property for longer, I would have made a bigger profit on the sale. Purchased for £138,000, it would now be worth upwards of £300,000. But you have to do what is right for you at the time. And, importantly, you learn lessons.

My first experience of buying a property through an auction was also a learning experience. Now, it is possible to secure some real bargains in the auction room. Most people sell their houses and apartments through estate agents and it can take months. An auction enables a quick sale, but often at a lower-than-market-value price. Often, a property will be listed because it has been repossessed by a bank. Perhaps the owner has defaulted on mortgage payments over a period of time, so the lender takes charge and puts it up for auction. Again, the aim is to achieve a rapid sale, even at the cost of a lower asking price.

Auction rules

So going to a property auction can be a great way to acquire property – either for rental or refurbishment and sale – but you have to be aware of the rules and how they can affect you.

In my case, I purchased an apartment. The next step was to secure a mortgage and that required a survey. Unfortunately, the survey valued the apartment at zero. It was apparently worth nothing because of some structural work – underpinning, to be precise – that had been done.

Now in theory this shouldn't have been too much of a problem. The underpinning had been successful, and all I had to do was commission an additional survey to confirm the building was structurally sound. But the clock was ticking. The auction process gives you a limited period of time to pay the seller. Everything was winding down for the Christmas/New Year holiday period, and no one would do the necessary work for me. Meanwhile, the seller was telling me I was in default. As such, he was entitled to walk away with my 10 per cent deposit.

Fortunately, he gave me the option of paying a second 10 per cent to keep the deal alive. I had to do that to avoid losing everything but the stress was too much. The mortgage came through, but I put the property in the next auction. I got my money back and moved on.

So am I saying stay clear of auctions? Absolutely not. They do work. I bought another auctioned property for £105,000 and sold it for £140,000. You really can make it work for you.

Here's what I've learned. First and foremost, you have a short window within which to work – effectively you have six to eight weeks to complete the deal. That's not difficult if it's a cash purchase, but if a mortgage is required, then you need to be sure that everything can be completed in the timeframe.

So, before you proceed, carry out checks on the property – or, to put it another way, make sure you do your due diligence. This is time-consuming but necessary. If you don't undertake as much checking upfront, it's perfectly possible that you will get lucky, strike a great deal and all will be fine. But on the other hand, you can be blown out of the water.

Remember also to set aside money to pay the auction fees, which usually come in at around 5 per cent. Otherwise, you could blow your budget.

If you are new to buying at auctions, there will always be unknown unknowns – things you don't plan for simply because you aren't aware you have to. I would recommend speaking to a professional adviser or to people who have spent a lot of time buying property in auction rooms.

But let's fast-forward to 2022 when Bianca sourced a distressed property in south-east London for £228,000 with a market value of £280,000. This required £70,000 worth of upfront costs with a mortgage cost of £533 and a rental income of £1,350, giving us a healthy monthly return. We plan to keep this property for at least the next five years and either remortgage to release equity or sell to return a profit, depending on our circumstances and requirement for capital at that time. This might not be the norm but it is achievable. Once you've scouted out the territory, property is a sound investment.

Learning the ropes

In fact, if you see property not simply as a means to invest some cash to secure a side income but rather as a profession, it is often a good idea to undertake a formal education process.

Certainly, that's the view of Alfred Dzadey, an award-winning property developer from England's West Midlands region. We spoke to him to get his expert view on the opportunities in the market.

An engineer by training, Alfred was carving out a good career as a project manager at Jaguar Land Rover when the opportunity arose to switch careers and move into the world of professional property development.

'I was doing well. I was earning around £60,000 a year from my salary but I wanted to build wealth. I looked around and saw that property was in most people's portfolios. It seemed like a good investment,' he says.

Alfred decided to learn about the industry from others, opting for a paid education. That gave him the grounding and knowledge he needed to pursue his ambitions. As he acknowledges, there was a lot to learn, not just about the property market but also about how finance is raised. 'When I started, I didn't know how money worked. I didn't know how mortgages worked,' he says.

But you can learn. The bigger point here is that you can never acquire too much information and there are various routes available. Alfred used an education company. In my case, I began going to auctions when I was still at university and spoke to professionals in the industry. And, as I've mentioned, financial and property advisers will always be happy to talk through your investment decisions and strategies.

By educating yourself and talking to experts, you fill in the gaps in your own knowledge. As Alfred puts it: 'You don't know what you don't know. So you sit in the right rooms with the right people who know more than you.'

Wealth creation through property remained nothing more than an ambition until Alfred lost his job as a contract worker for Jaguar Land Rover during the pandemic. 'Because I had invested in my education, I didn't even think about applying for a job. I had the knowledge and the networks, so I went into property full-time. I started my first project in 2020,' he recalls.

With an education to underpin his plans, Alfred undertook ambitious projects from the outset. His approach was to buy family homes and convert them into houses in multiple occupation, often abbreviated to HMOs.

Technically speaking, an HMO is a property rented out by at least three tenants forming more than one household. Usually, a conversion to an HMO enables the rental yield from a property to be higher than would be the case under a single occupation, simply because two flats/apartments will earn more than one house.

That sounds simple enough, but multiple skills are required. First and foremost, you need enough market and financial knowledge to build a sustainable business plan. How much will the property cost and how will you acquire it? How will it be financed? What will the conversion cost? What can you expect in terms of rental income and thus the return on the investment?

On top of that, there are all the skills required to convert the property. Some people do all the work themselves or rope in friends, but if it's a big project it's more likely that the services of builders, electricians, plumbers and decorators will all have to be paid for and their work managed to avoid the project going over budget.

That's where Alfred's previous background as a project manager in the automotive industry was invaluable. His strength was in managing the work of others, and his first project was completed in close to the allotted time.

As he recalls, his first project involved diving in at the deep end. 'A lot of refurbishment was needed,' he says.

And there were a number of challenges to overcome, many of them related to materials. 'But I was big on teams,' he says. 'My team were solutions-oriented and we found clever ways to get around things. The job was scheduled for four months; actually, it took five.'

As anyone who has undertaken refurbishment work will tell you, that kind of overrun represents a pretty good result, particularly in the case of a first project.

The location factor

Regardless of your investment strategy, one thing you must consider very carefully is the location of the property you're planning to buy.

Location affects the value of a property, not just in terms of how much it will cost to acquire but also the rental prospects and the potential for profit when the time comes to sell.

So what does that mean in practice? Well, all things being equal a property close to a good range of amenities – such as shops, a railway station, decent restaurants, schools and possibly a community hub – is going to be worth more than one that is less well connected. The quality of the neighbourhood also matters. A well-tended house or apartment in a smart street is likely to be much more valuable than a similarly attractive dwelling surrounded by boarded-up buildings. In the case of houses, the land footprint a property sits on also has an influence on value. Usually the bigger the footprint, the higher the sale price.

On the other hand, the proximity of a busy road is likely to reduce the value as will a badly maintained interior or exterior.

The value of a property will also depend on the average cost of housing in a particular city or region. In the UK, property in London will, typically, be much more expensive per square foot than its counterpart in a small town within a less economically developed region. It's the same everywhere. Property in Manhattan, Brooklyn or Queens is going to be more expensive than in places such as Hornell in upstate New York. These variations are a fact of life.

To take a couple of examples. According to UK government statistics, at the time of writing, the average cost of a home in London was £545,000. This compared with £168,000 in the north-east of England, the cheapest area.

There can be considerable variations within cities. The New York City real-estate consultant PropertyClub recently reported that, while houses in Brooklyn averaged $900,000, you could pick something up in Inwood, Manhattan, for $300,000 to $600,000. It is considered the last affordable district in New York.

High valuations are not necessarily a good thing for investors who plan to rent out their properties. What really matters is the relationship between the cost of the property and the rental income it can command. A property bought relatively cheaply and rented out for £1,000 a month is more attractive than a significantly more expensive dwelling that would nonetheless generate roughly the same monthly revenue.

That's one of the attractions of auctions – they reduce the purchase costs. It's also a factor that encourages some investors to look beyond their home areas to find places where property values are low and rents relatively high.

For instance, an investor based in London might look at prices in the Midlands city of Wolverhampton and think: 'That's where I'm going to invest.'

It's certainly a workable strategy, but caution is required. If you don't know an area well, it's very difficult to judge the investment potential of a property. In your own town and city, you probably know which streets are considered desirable and those which are up and coming. Equally, you probably have a pretty good handle on the less desirable districts.

That's much harder to determine if the property in question is 500 miles away in an unfamiliar city. You can look at pictures, but they won't tell you what the other houses look like. You can search property values and average rents by postcode but that can be misleading. A single postcode can hide a considerable variation in valuations. And what you won't necessarily see are the very local indicators of value and – perhaps more importantly – the ability to attract high-quality tenants. As Alfred puts it: 'One street can be great. The next one – well, no one wants to live there.'

So, if your plan is to buy in a location where you can get more for your money, you should be prepared to travel to the location and spend some time there assessing the house or apartment and its surroundings. Ideally, you would see the street in the daytime and after dark. Equally, you should spend some time understanding the rental market in the area. Who will the property be attractive to – students, young professionals, families – and how much will they pay? This is another aspect of due diligence.

You should also consider what an out-of-area purchase will mean for your own time. Will you have to make regular 200-mile round trips to sort out a problem? Yes, you will probably employ managing agents, but they are unlikely to do everything for you. It may be much easier to focus on properties close to home.

Think about what you are looking for financially. Buying cheap might offer a higher yield from the rental but you could miss out on gains made from the appreciation of the property when the time comes to sell. Do you need income now, or is the goal to take a big profit further down the line?

It's also important to think about the target tenants. Young single professionals tend to have different requirements from married couples or families. The former may want something small and close to bars, nightclubs, theatres and cinemas. They may not mind a rail line close by. A young couple could have similar requirements but be looking for square footage. If it's a family, the goal is probably either a large apartment or a house with a garden. Proximity to nightclubs might not be high on their list of priorities.

Alfred has a very focused strategy. 'I invest in city centres,' he says. 'When people move to a city that's where they want to live.' It's an approach focused on developing property around proven market demand. It's almost, but not quite, a hard-and-fast rule. 'I would only consider developing property further out of town if it was around a hospital,' he says. Again, demand is the key – doctors, nurses, physios and a host of other health workers looking for accommodation close to their places of work.

Finance options

The big question mark hanging over all property projects relates to finance. Investing in any kind of property – whether it's a house for straightforward rental to tenants to tenants via an HMO (house in multiple occupancy) conversion or something that involves major building work – requires a considerable capital outlay. Very few people will start their investment careers with enough money in the bank to simply go out and buy their chosen project. Consequently, funding will be required.

As Alfred observes, the need to raise money needn't be a stumbling block. 'Not everyone has their own capital,' he says. 'But you can create capital. You can leverage capital from banks, institutions and credit cards.'

Just how you access the necessary finance will depend on your own circumstances and the nature of the project, but there are a number of options available, including friends and family investment, buy-to-let mortgages and development loans.

The simplest option is to take out a mortgage. Conventional mortgages are designed to help people who want to buy homes to live in. If you're buying a house to rent to someone else, a specialist loan – known in the UK as a buy-to-let mortgage – is required.

Banks usually make the distinction for a very good reason. When someone takes out a conventional home loan, they will typically live in the property, maintain it carefully (it's normally their biggest asset) and move heaven and earth to make the monthly payments on time. The loan is granted because the prospective homeowner has sufficient income to honour the repayments. As part of the application process, the bank will also take a view on whether changing circumstances – such as a rise in interest rates – could make it difficult for the buyer to meet the repayment obligations.

In the case of a commercial mortgage, the perceived risk is greater. Buyers may be already paying a mortgage on their own homes. That doesn't leave a lot of spare income to make repayments on a second property, unless it is covered by the rental income. As any landlord will tell you, tenants can be unpredictable. They might move out suddenly or be slow in paying the rent. This can create a cash-flow problem.

So, typically, interest rates on homes-to-rent loans will be higher than would be the case with conventional mortgages. The deposits required by lenders also tend to be larger.

But there's an upside. The cost of purchasing the property can be factored into the rent. Any increase in interest rates can also be factored in when the lease comes up for renewal. It's important to ensure, however, that the rent a property can command in a given area will more than cover the mortgage payments.

Finance becomes slightly more complex in the case of property refurbishment and/or conversion. You can certainly get a mortgage on, say, a house that is being broken up into flats, but that won't be available until the work is done and the newly minted apartments are ready for rental or resale.

In these situations, you may require a bridging loan. Put simply, this is a short-term debt that enables you to cover the cost of buying and converting a property. Once the work is done, the loan can either be paid off by the sale of the dwelling or by taking out a mortgage. The full loan plus interest is paid at the end of the process. Bridging loans are most appropriate for projects that take very little time to complete, say weeks or a few months. Longer projects mean more interest having to be paid. However, some lenders will provide long-term bridging finance.

For those with more ambitious property development plans, the solution is often development finance that covers the cost of building houses, apartments or offices from the ground up. Broadly speaking, this kind of funding covers the purchase of land and a percentage of the actual building costs, with money released in tranches as the work progresses.

Now, those are some of the options available from commercial lenders. You may also be able to secure at least some of the capital you need from friends, family or business partners. In most cases, they will want a return. For example, if a family member helps out with conversion costs, the return could come through a share of the rental income or the profits of a sale.

The important thing to remember is that all of the above funding options have been designed for fairly specific purposes. Before setting out to raise capital, it's important to do your research and decide on the most appropriate source.

The prospect of raising finance – particularly if it involves large amounts of money through unfamiliar loan structures – can seem daunting. It's easy to be deterred by a feeling that borrowing at the kind of level needed to purchase a house or apartment for commercial reasons is something that other people do. The bank, you might conclude, will simply say no.

But everyone has to start from somewhere. Provided you make your business case, banks and other investors see property as a relatively safe proposition. Underpinning the loans is the fact that land and property have a value that can be recovered.

Nevertheless, banks won't back you unless they feel you are creditworthy and credible. The same is true of other investors.

'People will want to know what your principles are. They will want to know you. Trust you. And they will also have to like the project,' says Alfred. So what makes an investor like a project? Well, as Alfred sees it, it is about weighing up the required investment against the returns. 'They will want to see a fair exchange of value,' he adds. 'If you can tick these boxes, you will be able to raise capital.'

That's the theory. But how do you set about ticking those boxes in practice? Let's assume for a moment that you have a good or decent credit score. That's a positive start, but it doesn't provide any evidence of acumen in business. From an investor point of view, in the early days of your career you are likely to be a blank sheet. You have something to prove.

One way forward is to build a reputation. In Alfred's case, the starting point was demonstrating that he was someone who could deliver a return on investors' money – initially in the events market. For investment, he initially turned to friends and family.

'Working in the events business made me realize that I could raise money. I started small with £5,000 and £10,000 raises. That was when I had no track record. By making money for investors, I got to the stage where I was raising £50,000.'

At that point, Alfred decided to move into property. The financial cost of entry was higher, but even if the sums required were larger he saw property as a surer prospect than events. 'The events market was much riskier,' he says. 'You can hit a situation where an artist doesn't turn up and you lose your investment.'

Another factor was the desire for a means to grow wealth. An event doesn't in itself leave any legacy of wealth creation. You run an event and take the profit and that's it. In contrast, Alfred saw property as a means to create wealth by building a portfolio of assets that would appreciate in value over time.

And, by that stage, potential investors were more willing to put in larger sums. 'They said, "Yes, we know you. We know what you can do."' Crucially, they were also content to accept a slower return.

As Alfred acknowledges, building a reputation in the eyes of investors requires a degree of self-belief. 'It's all about having confidence in your own business plan, even when others have yet to be convinced. There are always doubters. My self-belief enabled me to do what I was doing while dismissing negative opinions,' he says.

Even today, Alfred takes the management of his reputation very seriously. He is active on social media, publicizing his projects and achievements. To put it another way, he has established a brand that can be built upon. His next step is to establish a property investment fund. This will enable him to grow a much bigger portfolio while making returns for investors.

Scale is important. As he explains, the rental return from one or two properties might provide an income of £2,000 a month. By growing the portfolio, a developer can aggregate income from a range of properties. 'There's a prospect of making £50,000 or £100,000 a month. That really excites me,' he says.

It's important to choose the right investors. It's a complex rela-tionship. Anyone with money to commit to a project will be seeking a return, but behind that simple statement of fact there is a huge amount of complexity. Every investor is different. Some will be seek-ing high returns, either rapidly or over a period of time. Others look for safe and secure investments that will provide a reliable income. Some will have £10,000 to commit, others £100,000. Each investor will have a very personal tolerance for risk.

So if you are seeking funding from friends or family investment at one end of the spectrum or wealthy individuals – often character-ized as high net worths – at the other, it is important to understand them. 'I always talk to them,' says Alfred. 'I try to find out who they are. Do they have kids? What motivates them? Have they invested before? I try to work out what kind of figure they are going to be comfortable with.'

'The next step is to say, "This is what I can offer you. Do you want to invest?" Essentially, I present them with an opportunity which solves a problem they have. That is how I raise capital.'

Not everyone reading this book will harbour empire-building ambitions, but whatever you aim for – be it a single buy-to-let prop-erty or a large portfolio, the principle is the same. While the capital requirements are considerable, the sources of finance are available and what you end up with is an income and asset that can be sold.

Marketing your property

Once you've secured your finance, purchased a property and got it ready to rent out or sell, the next step is to find tenants or buyers.

This is something that should be done as quickly as possible. If you're paying a mortgage, money will be going out of your bank account with none coming in until you get the tenants through the door and settled in. The same principle applies to reselling.

One potential problem for those who buy-to-let is that you can't really market a property until you own it and have the keys in your hand. The sale is complete, the mortgage payments kick in, and your challenge is to find suitable tenants quickly.

Fortunately, there is a huge demand for accommodation. Indeed, there is a shortage, so you shouldn't have too much of a problem finding a tenant. The best course of action is to use an estate agency/realtor with experience in renting out houses and apartments in your chosen area.

If the property has been purchased via a bridging loan – to be converted into a mortgage on completion of refurbishment or conversion – you can begin to market it before the work is completed. Put simply, you already own it. The challenge is to ensure that tenants are in place once the mortgage payments fall due.

For his part, Alfred always begins marketing towards the end of the conversion project, not after. That way there are tenants ready to move in when all the work has been done.

Once tenants are in situ, it only remains to ensure that the rent and service charges are paid and there is a choice to be made here. Either, you opt to do all the administration work yourself or you appoint a managing agent. An agent might charge up to 20 per cent of monthly income, although there are cheaper options.

An agent does more than simply collect the rent. They will liaise with tenants on the various issues that come up over the course of a leasing agreement. This could include dealing with any repairs that need to be made. They should also ensure the property is well maintained over the course of the tenancy. In addition, they will handle the paperwork and administration, including the renewal of leases.

As a landlord, you may have to get involved personally at times – for instance, if money needs to be spent to fix a broken boiler or faulty electrics – but the agent acts as both an administrator and a buffer between owner and tenant. They should also be experts in handling all the legal issues associated with managing tenancies. Before you choose an agent, it's always a good idea to talk to them about their experience and perhaps also seek testimonials from other landlords who have used them.

For that reason, many landlords will choose to use agents, but it is a personal decision.

In fact, just about every aspect of property investment comes down to personal decision making and you always have to ask what is right for you at any given time.

Let me take an example. Let's assume for a moment that your strategy is to rent houses or apartments to tenants. In order to do that, you take out one or more mortgages or – as Alfred has done – take out bridging loans to provide conversion finance in the first instance.

That's great, but where do you live? Are you also paying a mortgage on your own home? Certainly, that's what a lot of buy-to-let landlords do. But there are alternatives. You could buy a family home, rent it out and use a percentage of the monthly income to rent a smaller apartment for yourself.

There are some advantages to this approach. You are focusing your investment on the rental property while, perhaps, keeping your own costs under control. For instance, if you decide to rent a furnished flat for yourself, you won't have to spend money buying beds, sofas and the rest. Neither will you be tempted to build extensions, knock down walls or do a root-and-branch redecoration. This is a strategy favoured by Alfred.

Alternatively – and we touched on this earlier – you might not even buy a property. You might instead rent from a landlord who doesn't mind you subletting to other tenants or managing a high-value holiday lets business, facilitated by Airbnb or something similar.

My own view is that whatever model you adopt, you should own at least one property. Yes, rent it out if that's appropriate for your circumstances, but as long as you hold the deeds, you have a valuable long-term asset that can be sold in the future.

It's important to remember that, even if you don't go into the property business, the house or apartment that you own has huge value. It will appreciate over time. It can be remortgaged to raise capital – if, say, you need money to start a business. It can be passed on to your children, creating generational wealth. It can even serve as a pension pot if you choose either to downsize from a large to a smaller home or explore accessing capital through equity release.

Whether or not you choose to do any of these things, the property you live in is an asset that provides a degree of stability and security, particularly so when the mortgage is paid off and you have somewhere to live that costs nothing, except for maintenance costs and local taxes.

So whether you buy property to generate income or simply to have somewhere to live, what I would say is simply this: the best time to invest is today. But, crucially, understand your own requirements. Study the market. Assess the risk. And choose the most appropriate finance option.

Alfred Dzadey's top tips for property investment

- Invest in your education. You don't know what you don't know.
- Surround yourself with active property investors – you become who you surround yourself with!
- Get clear on your strategy and stick to that one strategy. Become a master at that one thing before diversifying.
- Study the market to see what is working and replicate what works – for example what types of rental are being rented quickly.
- Location is everything when it comes to property investment – do not compromise on this just to get a deal done.
- We get into property investment for income and not to work for the income, so create systems and processes so that your role is as passive as possible.
- If you are wanting to scale your property business, you need to learn how to raise capital so you can accelerate your growth!
- Do not scale until you have gone through the entire process. In this way, you can implement your lessons learned and make the process more efficient.
- When starting out looking for people to invest in your projects, you have to start from your immediate circle (e.g. your family, friends and work colleagues).
- Always be a student of the game – the minute you think you know it all is when things start to go downhill.

The Rich Forever checklist

- Assess your financial situation and determine your budget for buying a property by speaking to a broker. Secure financing through a mortgage or other loan, if necessary.
- Research properties that meet your needs and preferences, including location, size and amenities. Work with an estate agent to help you find properties that match your criteria. Don't panic buy – the right property will come along!
- Negotiate the purchase price with the seller based on the property's condition, market value, and other factors.
- Hire a professional home inspector to evaluate the property and identify any issues or concerns that may affect its value or safety.
- Hire a property lawyer/real estate attorney to review the purchase agreement, provide legal advice, and facilitate the closing process.
- Review the property documents, including the title, deed, survey and other relevant records, to ensure that there are no charges/liens, encumbrances or other legal issues that could affect your ownership or use of the property.
- Obtain homeowner's insurance to protect your property against damage, theft or other risks.
- Close the deal. Attend the closing meeting to sign the purchase agreement, transfer ownership, and make the final payment.
- Arrange for the transfer of utilities, address changes, and any necessary repairs or renovations, and move in/lease your new property.

Remember, property is about building wealth in the long term. In most instances it requires large amounts of capital and has a low return in the short term.

This checklist is not exhaustive, and you may need to add or modify items based on your specific situation and needs.

CHAPTER EIGHT
Invest Small, Win Big – Alternative Investments

'How many millionaires do you know who have become wealthy by investing in savings accounts?' (Robert G. Allen); our answer would be zero and we know a fair number of million- and billionaires. Let's say you have some money in a savings account, a portfolio of shares and perhaps an investment property or two. Assuming you've also got a decent income and sufficient insurance to ensure your loved ones are provided for in the event of death or serious illness, your financial management basics are more or less covered.

But what if you've got some additional money set aside for investment and you want to do something a bit different? Maybe you'd like to allocate some of the available cash to higher-return investments. Perhaps you'd simply like to have some fun and turn a passion into an income stream.

This is the point when many people start to consider alternative investments – opportunities to secure returns from assets that sit outside the financial market mainstream.

Anything that gains value over time or provides an income can be considered an 'investment'. Or, to put it another way, your investment strategy doesn't have to be limited to the 'usual suspects' of shares and property. In fact, there are countless opportunities to preserve and grow your wealth across a range of asset classes. Some are well known, others surprising.

So what do we mean by alternative investments?

It's actually a pretty loose term that can cover anything from investment in gold, silver or esoteric financial vehicles – such as hedge or private equity funds – to the buying and selling of tangible items, such as paintings, wine, watches or boxed toys from previous eras. The common factor is a distance from the beaten track.

Purely from a financial perspective, alternative investments are well worth considering. If you make good choices, they can offer a higher return on your money than some of the more mainstream options.

They also provide a means to diversify your investment portfolio and protect your wealth in the event of, say, a downturn in the share markets or a blip in the property sector.

Low correlation

For instance, you might choose an alternative asset class because it has – as financial advisers are keen to tell you – a low correlation to other assets. In somewhat plainer English, this means that some alternative assets have a tendency to gain value at times when bad economic news pushes shares down and puts a cap on property prices. To take an example, gold prices tend to perform well when economies go into recession. Thus, many professional investors will include gold in their portfolios.

Then there is the fun factor. In addition to alternative investments that are to some extent adjacent to the mainstream financial markets, others sit well outside. Often, these are tangible items including:

- wine
- antiques
- art
- sought-after luxury goods, such as watches and handbags
- collectables such as vintage toys (usually in their original boxes) and trading cards
- classic cars …

That's just a taster — there are many more.

So an alternative investment strategy might be triggered by an interest in assets such as treasury bonds that are off-the-beaten-track as far as most investors are concerned. Or you could be drawn to invest in something you are passionate or knowledgeable about. The common factor is the potential — and we are, I stress, talking about potential — to deliver better-than-average returns if you make the right calls.

Part I: Financial alternatives

Let's first have a look at alternative investments that are essentially financial in nature. And by that I mean they can be bought and sold either through online financial services trading platforms or via financial advisers and brokers.

For instance, the commodities market has become increasingly popular in recent years. There can be big fluctuations in commodities prices, opening the door to high returns but also serious losses.

Commodities is a catch-all term that covers physical assets that are traded on international and local markets. Gold and silver are commodities as are base metals such as nickel, lead and zinc. Oil and gas are also commodities along with foodstuffs.

Commodities can be attractive because they often have a negative correlation — those words again — with the direction of the wider economy. The shortage of a particular commodity — let's say oil — can push economies into recession — while owners of the oil make enormous profits. We saw this during the war in Ukraine when oil supplies came under pressure and the big suppliers recorded record profits. Meanwhile, the economies of Europe and North America were being dragged down by rapidly rising prices.

Investing in commodities is not difficult to do. You can buy shares of companies working in the sector. Alternatively, you can invest in an exchange-traded fund (ETF) or in a mutual fund that specializes in the commodities sector.

But I would advise caution. In January 2023 the *Financial Times* noted that retail investors (just about anyone who isn't a professional trader) were increasingly attracted to the commodities market, despite warnings that volatile prices could result in heavy losses. These are difficult markets if you're not an expert.

Gold

However, some corners of the commodities are accessible and, on the face of it, offering a fairly safe haven for spare investor cash.

Gold is a case in point. It is another negative correlation commodity. When shares and currencies lose value, investors often turn to gold, pushing its price up.

In the UK, you can simply visit the Royal Mint website and buy gold bullion (www.royalmint.com/invest/). In the USA, you can visit your preferred precious metals exchange. It's as simple as providing your details and making a payment.

But maybe not quite that simple. If you buy a bar of gold, you either have to store it yourself – creating security issues – or pay someone else to look after it for you. You probably don't want to have, say, a kilo of gold in your house. It could be worth something in the region of £40,000 per kilo. That's about the same weight as a bag of sugar, making it very easy for a thief to simply put it in a bag and walk out the door. It's not wise to use it as a doorstop, although I joke with Bianca all the time about doing so.

Alternatively, the Royal Mint sells digital gold, which is backed up by the physical asset stored in a safe location.

That's what Bianca and I opted for, with mixed results. Gold is considered a safe bet but it's not necessarily a ticket to riches. Although the value of gold has risen significantly on international markets, that hasn't been reflected in our holding. In fact, our gold has gained only a minute amount. Frustratingly, most of the profit has been eaten up by VAT (value-added tax) and we are also being charged for storage. I don't know why we are being charged for storing digital gold, but we are.

The question is, then: is gold a good investment? A quick check of spot prices per ounce over the last ten years tells a story of fluctuating prices. In 2013 an ounce was priced at around $1,600. From there it dipped below $1,500 until 2019. At the time of writing it stood at $1,800. Those who bought in during the low period have done relatively well. Those with investments dating back to 2013 have made some gains. Investors coming into the market in 2021 (the high point) have made small losses.

And as Bianca and I have discovered, increases in the spot price may not be reflected in your own portfolio and there are the associated fees to consider.

Nevertheless, gold can be a good investment. You are unlikely to lose your shirt as it will always be stable, but have sensible expectations. It's relatively safe and can sometimes deliver impressive returns.

Real estate

Real estate is well worth considering. We've talked a lot about residential property in this book – mostly in terms of houses and apartments that can be bought, rented and sold using bank cash to support the investment. But there is a wider world of real estate investment covering big residential projects (the construction of apartments and houses) and commercial properties such as shopping malls and office blocks.

Anyone can invest in real estate through managed funds – known as real estate investment trusts (REITs) in the UK. These give exposure not just to the domestic market but also to overseas property developments. For instance, there are huge property development opportunities in emerging markets such as Africa and in the United Arab Emirates (UAE).

The good news is that overseas investors are often welcomed. For instance, the UAE offers major investors an investor visa, allowing them to set up a home and business in the country along with family members. The visa is available to those investing AED (the Emirates dirham) 1 million (about £215,000 or $272,000) and illustrates just how keen the UAE authorities are to attract overseas investment.

Peer-to-peer lending

Online platforms have changed the investment landscape in the last 15–20 years, not least by allowing investors to buy shares or trade in foreign currencies relatively easily.

One particularly interesting development has been the proliferation of peer-to-peer lending platforms.

Put simply, these sites enable investors to pool their money and lend either to individuals or small businesses who need cash. The platforms carry out due diligence on the creditworthiness of borrowers and interest rates are usually set in line with the perceived risk. You commit money for a period of time. The interest rate return can be anything between (a low) 1 per cent and 6 per cent. The percentage is usually fixed and is dependent on how long you leave your money in the pot.

The first peer-to-peer lending site in the UK was Funding Circle but others quickly followed. Some specialize in lending to specific sectors, such as property.

This form of investment is not quite as safe as putting your money in a bank savings account. Although borrowers are credit-checked, economic slowdowns, recessions and adverse market conditions can affect the ability of small businesses and individuals to repay their loans. Thus. committing money to these platforms does expose you to a degree of risk. The returns, however, are higher than would be expected from a bank savings account.

Foreign exchange

The attraction of the foreign exchange (FX or forex) market is very similar to that of commodity trading. Essentially, this is about buying and selling currencies as they shift in value in relation to one another. If the dollar moves up in value, an investor holding the US currency can sell at a profit. The movement of currencies can be considerable. For instance, in the immediate aftermath of the Brexit vote, the pound fell 16 per cent as currency traders sold sterling. In cases like this, the money tends to go somewhere else – notably into US dollars and euros – pushing up the value of these other currencies. This creates opportunities to make money by buying a currency as it goes down and selling on the upswing.

Bianca and I have always had an interest in forex trading. In fact, the first time we did any training together was in 2011, when we paid a fee to learn how to invest in currencies. It cost £1,500, which seemed like a fortune at the time. We went to the coach's own residence – a beautiful house with some lovely cars outside – and he showed us how to trade.

And I have to say it isn't that easy. Bianca and I decided there was no pathway for us. Since then we've had other people trade currencies on our behalf, but it is risky. One of the most commonly quoted statistics is that 95 per cent of would-be forex traders lose their entire pot in the first six months. There is actually very little research to back this up, but it has become something of a financial industry benchmark. Some would say the losses are even greater.

The problem may be that forex is often perceived as a fast track to rapid profits. That perhaps encourages people who don't have sufficient experience or knowledge to trade recklessly. What's more, if you spend any time on social media, you'll probably be confronted by ads offering courses in forex trading. The trainers will typically talk up the opportunities and rewards as evidenced by their own opulent lifestyles.

So here's the question. If you're tempted by the big money that can undoubtedly be made by experienced traders, how are you going to beat the odds? Even with training why will you be in the lucky 5 per cent?

When people tell me about forex and tell me it's an incredible thing, my spider senses start to tingle. I look at their branding and their track record.

Personally, I have always lost money on forex. I'm done with it. I won't be entering that market again. It's like gambling but with worse odds.

There are certainly other financial asset classes you can try, ranging from hedge funds – which promise to protect against risk – to farmland and agriculture. You can even invest in royalties in music and authorship. For instance, there are platforms that allow you to buy the rights to other people's music and earn royalties from stream and record sales. The artists or publishers sell their rights to generate upfront cash. The rights are traded online.

Investing in business

Investing in a small- or medium-sized business can be hugely satisfying, not least because you may be playing a material role in helping that company achieve its potential.

There are many ways to do this. Investing directly as a family or friends investor is perhaps the most common route. Essentially, if you know someone who needs capital, you can either lend the money or take a share in the company in exchange for cash. However, even if we are talking about genuine 'friends' and 'family', it's important to ensure that all the paperwork is in place covering the terms and conditions attached to the loan or shareholding. Nothing sours a friendship more than a dispute over money.

More formally, you might join an angel syndicate and invest in promising companies in your local area and beyond. These will normally be at an early stage, and, if they succeed, the value of the shareholding will grow, allowing you to sell your holding at a profit as part of the syndicate. You might also consider committing cash to a venture capital (VC) fund. The fund managers will invest in start-up companies on your behalf.

Investment in start-ups is risky. According to industry analyst Startup Genome, 90 per cent of start-ups fail. When that happens, shareholders lose everything they have invested. The advantage of pooling money with others through a VC fund is that the fund's managers will make investments across a range of companies on the basis that, while most will fail, the few that succeed will more than compensate.

As businesses grow and become well established, they are often bought out by private equity companies. Their aim is to take already successful companies and make them grow even faster. You can take advantage of this market by investing in a private equity (PE) fund.

According to the US Private Equity Index, PE funds produced an average annual return of 10.8 per cent between 2000 and 2020, outpacing the S&P 500 index and returns from VC funds.

There's also scope to invest in businesses at the very earliest stage. Over the past ten years, we've seen increasing numbers of people putting a toe in the business investment market through equity crowdfunding sites. Designed initially to appeal to fans of programmes such as *Shark Tank* (in the US) and its British equivalent, *Dragons' Den*, these sites allow individuals to commit relatively small amounts of money to early-stage companies in return for shares. The average investment through Crowdcube – the UK's longest-standing crowdfunding site – is £1,300. You can invest in much less than that – as little as £10 – but at that level you can't expect to make a huge amount of money.

National Savings

If you're looking for a very safe investment in the government bond market, national savings schemes offer an attractive entry point. For instance, the UK's National Savings & Investments (NS&I) markets both guaranteed growth bonds and premium bonds, with the latter paying out lottery-style cash prizes every month. Your money is safe and can be withdrawn at any time.

When Bianca went to university, she put a percentage of her maintenance loan into premium bonds, while doing a Saturday job to support herself. She hoped for a million-pound premium bond win. The largest amount she won was about £50 – doing so a few times over the years. My own wins have been around the £25 or £50 mark each time. Regardless of the savings options, I would recommend NS&I as a great savings option, especially as an alternative to leaving cash in a basic current account.

A small caveat. It's not necessarily a good idea to put your student maintenance loan into a savings and premium bond scheme, but Bianca was fortunate enough to have enough money to live on with something left over for investment.

Part II: Investing in tangibles

Now let's take a closer look at the market for tangible investments, such as art, luxury goods or wine. These are assets you can enjoy and some of them, if chosen well, deliver superior returns. It's important to stress, though, that buying and selling tangible items is not quite as straightforward as trading shares.

Art

Once you begin to look outside the world of finance, one of the most high-profile areas of alternative investment is art.

Now, a lot of people buy art simply for pleasure rather than as means to drive investment returns. What can happen, however, is that, as you become involved with the art world and gain knowledge and expertise, you begin to scout out opportunities to build a valuable investment portfolio.

The great thing about art is that you can buy a piece, put it in your home, look at it and enjoy it, and all the while it is appreciating in value.

And art does appreciate. The value of the global art market grew from $441 to $579.5 billion, an increase of 38 per cent, according to the Business Research Company.

Of course, that's a headline figure. Barely a year goes past without at least one news story highlighting a record-breaking sale of a painting, sculpture or (latterly) digital artwork. In 2022, Andy Warhol's *Blue Marilyn* sold for $195 million, making it the highest-selling artwork of the year. Also in 2022, art owned by Microsoft co-founder Paul Allen sold for $1.6 billion, with the top five paintings going for more than $100 million each. These figures illustrate just how much collectors and museums are willing to pay.

Those figures can also be extremely daunting. After all, very few people can afford to invest in a Monet, Picasso or Hockney. So can you find investible art that has a lower cost of entry?

The short answer is yes. My friend Marine Tanguy is CEO of art talent agency MTArt. As she points out, investing in art is a little bit like investing in a business. If it's a start-up, you can buy shares relatively cheaply but there is no guarantee of success. The business could fail, or it could become a world-beater. If it does succeed, early investors make a fortune.

Then there's the mid-tier. The business has a track record, backed up by data. The shares are more expensive but it's a safer bet.

Finally, to continue the analogy, there are the big corporations. Their shares go up and down, but usually not by very much. Investors know they are safe, stable companies that are generating enormous revenues. You rarely lose your shirt when you invest.

Apply that to the art world and you see similar tiers. There are the new artists without a real following; rising stars who have gained both a critical reputation and a following; and the big fish – people who can already sell their work for millions. The risk-and-reward profile is different for each of these. Buy the work of a talented new-comer for a few thousand pounds and it could be worth five or ten times that amount in a decade. Invest in a mid-tier artist and there is room for appreciation if their reputation grows further. Art by big names will probably at least hold their value and may grow strongly with the market as appetite for fine art rises. But the work is no longer affordable to most people.

So let's assume you're not in the market for Warhol or even a Banksy. How do you get a foothold in art investment by buying lesser-known artists with potential?

The first step is to seek professional advice. Talk to dealers or industry experts about trends within the industry and the artists whose work is affordable to you. Always check the credentials of your advisers. Some will be more knowledgeable than others. Choose art-ists whose work you enjoy. Regardless of whether or not the value rises, you will have something that enhances your life.

So let's fast-forward a few years. The works of art you have pur-chased have pride of place on your walls. They are old friends. And they are a lot more valuable than they were when you bought them. This is the point at which there may be a tension between collecting and investing. How do you decide if and when to sell?

According to Marine, most art is sold at times of transition or crisis – divorce, death and financial problems being common reasons. However, a collector may choose to sell to take profits at any time. The timing is very much down to the individual to decide. A rapid increase in the value of a particular work could provide an opportu-nity to secure a return and use the cash to buy more pieces. Alterna-tively, it could be that paintings on the wall remain there as part of a long-term legacy that can be passed on to the next generation.

Personally, I have bought art but not as yet with investment in mind. That's the next level for me, so I asked Marine for some ground rules.

Marine Tanguy's top tips for investing in art

- Love the art you buy. If you buy the work of young artists, their career may not take off but, if you love the work, then it is a good investment regardless of the financial outcome.
- If you don't love the work, pass and find something else.
- Read as much on the topic as possible.
- Compare notes with other people. It's always much more fun to explore the artwork with others.
- Check the credentials of advisers. The art world is not very well regulated. People can do courses and set themselves up as experts with very little experience behind them.
- Find people who are genuinely knowledgeable. Take their advice.
- When it comes to selling, your first port of call should be the reseller from whom you bought it. They will know and control the market. They can get the best price.
- Be as self-aware as possible when you make art investment decisions.

Investments you can enjoy

The same principle applies to a whole range of tangible products, such as high-end watches, handbags, classic cars and sneakers. You can admire them and enjoy the experience of wearing them while having the satisfaction of knowing they are collectable and very possibly rising in value.

My first foray into the world of luxury goods came in the form of a Rolex watch, given to me by my parents when I turned 21. Now if you're a parent, this is something you might want to think about.

A memorable gift to mark an event is always good. The added bonus is its potential to increase in value. Again, there are legacy opportunities.

Since then, I have purchased two Hermès 'Birkin' handbags. Now, the 'Birkin' and 'Kelly' bags (both produced by Hermès) have proven to be extremely investible. They outperform the S&P 500 and are considered a better investment than gold.

Buying my first 'Birkin' bag felt like a big moment. It felt like an entry to an echelon of society where the bag carries a certain weight.

But are they really good investments? Yes, they are. The bags themselves cost from £10,000 upwards, but I know that, if I want to sell mine, I'm likely to get far more than the original sum paid. Quite a lot more in fact. According to Credit Suisse and Deloitte, the investment return on a Chanel bag is 11.8 per cent. The return on a 'Birkin' is 38 per cent. The most expensive 'Birkin' sold for more than $300,000 at Sotheby's. They are perceived as pieces of art. Collectors flock to buy them,

For instance, the Canadian musician Drake has shelves full of them with values ranging from $40,000 to $500,000 each. It is a huge collection of rare bags. You can see this as a genuine part of your investment portfolio.

Watches

Let's take another example. Byron and I both own luxury Rolex watches and over the years we have seen those increase in value.

But you can enjoy wearing a Rolex watch, knowing that it will – at the very least – hold its value. Some appreciate some stay where they are.

For instance, about 15 years ago, Byron bought a vintage Rolex 'Air King' for £1,500. Now that watch is £3,500 retail, even though it is used. On another occasion, he wanted to buy an Audemars Piguet 'Royal Oak'. At the time, it was being sold for £20,000. Now it is worth £40,000.

These are big choices, even if you are making a good amount of money. When I bought my second Rolex, I had to really think about it carefully. There were other things I could have been spending my money on, so the question was: did I really want it? Sometimes you have to think of it as being like getting on the housing ladder. If collectable luxury goods interest you, there's a point where you have to take a leap and spend some money.

It helps to be passionate about the items you're collecting. If you are, say, really into sneakers, the chances are you will know the brands, be aware of the value of individual items, and understand what makes collectors tick. That knowledge will help you make good investment choices.

Being active in the market also provides you with opportunities. It's not always easy or totally straightforward to buy a high-end watch or handbag. The supply is limited and a lot of the brands will sell only to those who are known to them and on their waiting lists. That's in part where the exclusivity and value comes from.

So if you are out there buying and selling, you make yourself known. That might be as simple as establishing a rapport with a particular sales assistant who can get you deals. However, that might not be enough. Some brands won't sell to you unless you have already spent money with them. That's a bit of a catch-22, but you can build a portfolio with a brand by purchasing preloved items.

You can keep wearables locked away but that would be a shame not to enjoy them. However, carrying an expensive bag or wearing a luxury watch involves a certain level of anxiety. With handbags, I'm constantly looking around me for anyone who is getting too close while also checking the heavens for signs of rain.

So think about the practicalities. Will you carry the 'Kelly' and/or wear the Rolex? Is the item first and foremost an investment? Or is it a combination of the two?

Making choices

If investment in a collectable item is a part of your financial thinking, then you're going to have to make some financial choices.

Let's stick with bags for a moment. As consumers, we tend to choose our purchases on non-investment criteria – the colour, the style, the price and what the piece will say about us being just four of the possible drivers.

Looking at a bag as an investment changes the choice dynamic, at least to some extent. In addition to all the factors listed above, you are also asking yourself whether it will deliver a return if sold.

Now, on that basis, you could buy something that is very much in demand. At the backend of the process, when you come to sell, that might be a good thing. A popular and in-demand item will sell for more than something that attracts less interest.

But it will cost you more money upfront. So there is a decision to be made about how much you are prepared to spend against the likely sale price. You might actually make a smaller profit on a sought-after bag because, although it sells for a high sum, you've also paid a lot to get it.

An alternative is to choose something cheaper. It might not gain so much in value, but the return could, nonetheless, be higher. These can be quite difficult judgements to make, so it's really important to take time to understand the market. That's true of bags, sneakers, antiques, watches or any kind of tangible product with investment potential.

Another factor to consider is the saleability of the chosen invest-ment. In the case of conventional investments, such as stocks and shares, selling is relatively easy. You just fire up your app of choice and make the sale. Property can take longer and the process is more laborious, but there's a lot of demand out there and the mechanisms (notably estate agencies) are in place to help you make the sale.

Using networks

Collectable items are a bit different. In many cases, you can look up the value on a website or in an industry guide, but getting the market price depends on connecting with buyers who are prepared to part with the sum of money you hope to receive.

Ask yourself this: when it comes to selling something from your watch, jewellery or bag collection, do you have access to a network of potential buyers – people who have both an interest in the class of item and the money to spend? If you don't, then the chances are you're going to have to engage the services of a professional who can make the sale. That could be a dealer, a broker working in the appropriate marketplace or an auctioneer.

If that's the case, you need to think about how much the sale will cost. A reseller may well offer you much less than the market value in order to leave room for quite a hefty margin – as much as 30 to 35 per cent, in fact. That could wipe out your profit. An auction house will take a commission.

I know someone who runs a restaurant. She also has an extensive handbag collection. During the pandemic, she was trying to sell her 28-inch, black, crocodile Hermès 'Kelly' bag for £50,000. What she came up against was the need to have a network. Without one, it could be difficult to sell a piece at a time – more or less – of your choosing at the right price.

Then there is the matter of when to sell. As is the case with conventional investments, this is something you should think about. For instance, if you own shares that are going up in value, you'll have to make a decision: Do you hold and hope the share price keeps on rising? Do you wait until the stock hits a certain level and then cash in? Or do you hang on to the shares over the long term as a kind of rainy-day investment to be cashed in when required? The same choices apply to tangible items.

Byron tends to take the attitude that 'When it gets to X I'm out'. But you could equally view your luxury good collection as part of your legacy.

Seeking advice

But what if you are not yet an active player in the market but are nevertheless attracted to a particular alternative asset class – whether that be classic cars, vintage wine or antiques?

The best course of action is to seek advice from people who are acknowledged experts in their respective fields. If you have friends or family members with the right kind of knowledge, they will probably be more than happy to help. Equally, you can talk to dealers about their market There are also online courses available across a range of alternative assets.

Equally important, do your own homework. Most alternative assets support trade and consumer magazines that regularly cover market trends. Information is also available from books and websites.

There are many kinds of alternative investments and they can add a lot to your portfolio. But think carefully about what you are seeking to achieve and take time to understand the market.

The Rich Forever checklist

- Understand the risk-and-reward profile of your chosen investment class.
- Look at the success rate of investors (very low in the case of foreign exchange).
- Take advice from professionals.
- Consider whether selling an asset will be straightforward.
- Ask yourself why you are investing. In the case of tangible assets, is it to make money or to enjoy your purchases?

CHAPTER NINE
The Truth about Cryptocurrencies

You can't deny there's a buzz around cryptocurrencies and their investment potential. With varying distinct schools of thought, from venture capitalist Chamath Palihapitiya stating 'It's money 2.0, a huge, huge, huge deal' to Jamie Dimon, CEO of J.P. Morgan 'It's a fraud [and] worse than tulip bulbs.' There can be few people with even a passing interest in money that haven't heard of them and perhaps been intrigued by their investment potential.

They are covered regularly on television and in newspapers and magazines. You may also have heard about 'crypto' from friends or friends of friends. You might even have been told that investing in crypto is the way to get rich. On the other hand, there are plenty of stories about hopeful investors who have come away with their fingers well and truly burned.

So what is the truth about cryptocurrencies? What are they? Do they have any relevance to you? More importantly, should investment in one or more cryptocurrencies form part of your financial plan?

I first heard of the cryptocurrency concept when my partner in the property business rang me and said we were going to buy bitcoin. 'That's great,' I replied. 'When can we look at the property?'

That was a few years back and my lack of knowledge was excusable. Relatively few people were aware that bitcoin – the first of the cryptocurrencies – even existed. Even fewer knew anything about it. And only a tiny number of people were buying into the coin in the hope that its rising value would deliver a handsome return to their bank accounts.

The relatively low profile of bitcoin had an upside. When I first found out about it, you could buy a single bitcoin for around $400. By October 2021 the value of a single coin had risen to $60,000. For those who got in early, investment in the currency represented a bonanza.

Since then, quite a few people – namely those who bought when bitcoin was at its peak value – have seen the value of their investments drop. As I'm writing this, the online statistics website Statista is reporting that bitcoins are currently worth $20,000 each. Now, that has delivered a good return for those who bought early and the value of the asset may rise again. But this is a market that should be approached carefully.

So what exactly is cryptocurrency?

Well, there are currently thousands of different cryptocurrencies in circulation. Depending on whom you believe, the number is somewhere between 4,000 and 20,000.

The crypto world looked very different in 2009. That was the year that bitcoins were released onto computer networks. The intention was to create a digital currency that would operate independently of banks and the traditional financial system. It could do everything you might expect a conventional currency to do. You could buy goods and services and also take payments. And, of course, you could also purchase units of the currency as an investment. But these transactions would sit outside the banking and payment infrastructure. And initially, at least, this was an unregulated space.

That was made possible because of a new technology known as the distributed ledger – more commonly known as the blockchain.

Welcome to the blockchain

When conventional electronic currency is involved, every time you transfer cash from one bank account to another, the amounts are calculated and the transaction is administered by banks and payment services providers. These are part of the financial services infrastructure. Unless you're exclusively using cash – and even that probably comes from an ATM – you can't do very much, financially speaking, without the involvement of at least one bank.

In the case of cryptocurrencies, all transactions take place on a platform hosting a digital ledger. Every time a bitcoin owner sanctions a transaction – such as a payment – the ledger updates. There is no need for what is known in the trade as a trusted third party (a bank or patent provider) to administer the process. Each blockchain/ ledger does the transactional work and record keeping for the currency it supports.

So why is this a good thing? To many people, the invention of cryptocurrencies provides a means to escape the strictures of the overlapping political, banking and economic systems. For instance, while the values of bitcoin and other currencies go up and down, they are not (in theory) affected by the political decision making that moves national currencies.

Cryptocurrencies are not stored in banks, and for some people at least, being outside the financial system is seen to have advantages. For instance, if a bank collapses, big depositors can lose most of their savings. And bank crashes do happen. Witness the collapse of the financial system in 2008.

Since then, the rules governing banking have been tightened up but there are still vulnerabilities. In early 2023, when Silicon Valley Bank (SVB) suffered a run on deposits, the US government had to rush in to guarantee the funds of the high-tech companies that had money deposited. SVB's British arm also had to be rescued by means of a takeover by HSBC. Having a source of funds outside the banking system does have an appeal.

Of course, there are also hazards associated with cryptocurrencies. I'll be looking at those in more detail later in the chapter.

The birth of cryptocurrencies

The birth of the cryptocurrency concept is cloaked in a degree of mystery. What we know – or think we know – is that the creation of bitcoin can be, in large part, credited to Satoshi Nakamoto. In 2008 Nakamoto published a scientific paper outlining how a digital currency could be underpinned by a blockchain ledger. It's thought he is also responsible for developing the bitcoin. But here's the problem. Because Nakamoto is a pseudonym, we don't really know very much at all about the motives and intentions behind the currency.

Nevertheless, the idea took off. For the first few years, individual bitcoins were worth very little. It wasn't until 2011 that they achieved parity with the dollar. After that, however, they began to gain value very quickly.

That raises the question – touched on in Chapter 1 – of why any currency has value in the first place.

In the case of cryptocurrency there are two key factors. Number one, it has a utility. Those who own it can complete transactions. For some people at least, an added attraction is the fact that transactions can be executed away from the radar screens of banks, regulators and state authorities. And let's be honest, that has made some cryptocurrencies very attractive to groups of people you wouldn't necessarily want to be dealing with. For instance, if you run a company that is unlucky enough to be the victim of a ransomware attack – in which online criminals lock your computer files and demand money to reopen them – the chances are you will be asked to pay them in a cryptocurrency.

And then there is scarcity. The number of bitcoins in circulation – and this applies to other cryptocurrencies – is limited. Bitcoins can be created by individuals, but they can't simply be plucked out of thin air. In order to successfully 'mine' a bitcoin you have to solve a complex maths problem. In theory, anyone can mine their own bitcoins. In practice, the problem is so complex that the solution requires a huge amount of computer processing power. It's expensive and time-consuming. That fact alone limits the number of coins in circulation at any one time.

So, just as central banks maintain the value of their currencies by controlling the amount of money in the economy, software rules and processes are used to achieve much the same end in the crypto world.

Exchanges and wallets

It's very easy to get carried away by the cryptocurrency concept, and many people are genuinely excited by the prospect of a monetary system that owes nothing to nation-states, banks or regulators.

Actually, though, you don't get very far in the crypto space without signing up to a 'trusted' third party in the form of a currency exchange. You could characterize these as fulfilling a similar role to banks.

Put simply, exchanges provide a means to buy and sell cryptocurrencies. At its simplest, you can use an exchange to buy bitcoin. However, you might use the same exchange to sell bitcoin and buy another currency, such as Tether or Ethereum which exist on different platforms.

In that respect, you can think of these exchanges in much the same way that you would use a phone app to buy and sell shares. They are essentially intermediaries. They do all the heavy lifting when you trade your cyber currencies. Ideally, as with any financial service, you'll want an exchange with decently low fees and high securities.

Potentially, this is a minefield. There are a lot of exchanges vying for your business and it's not always easy to tell if they are safe to use.

Witness the collapse of FTX, an exchange founded by Sam Bankman-Fried, an entrepreneur who built a $16 billion fortune and has been seen in the company of luminaries such as former US president Bill Clinton and one-time UK prime minister Tony Blair. In November 2021, FTX filed for bankruptcy. According to press reports, the company's top 50 creditors were owed $3 billion. FTX wasn't the first exchange to collapse, and the chances are, it won't be the last. Bankman-Fried was later arrested for fraud.

An exchange going bust can be a disaster for two reasons. First, if the exchange is also storing your cryptocurrencies, you could, temporarily or permanently, lose everything. In the event of a bankruptcy, all the funds held by the exchange will be frozen, including yours.

That's not the case if you store your own currencies.

So how does this work? Well, in order to own bitcoins and other currencies, you'll also need a wallet. These can be downloaded as PC/laptop or mobile apps. There are two varieties. Using a hosted app means your bitcoins – essentially software information – are managed by a third party. Often that third party is the exchange. Self-custody wallets, on the other hand, enable you to store your own data. Self-custody saves you from the frozen fund scenario because you have control of the digital asset so you can't be locked out if an exchange collapses. But if you forget or lose a password, you could be in trouble.

Second, the failure of an exchange sends shockwaves through the cryptocurrency community. Many people may sell their coins, and thanks to the relationship between supply and demand, the value will fall. There was a big slump after the FTX bankruptcy.

Peaks and troughs

But even in more stable times, cryptocurrency values are – in a word much favoured by investment professionals – volatile. Unlike, say, shares, there is no underlying value to these assets. A share price might fall and investors can look at the performance of the company and assess whether the sell-off on the part of other investors was justified. If the company is actually performing well, a dip in the market might represent a good time to buy more shares in the business on the assumption the value will rise again. The investor might get the call wrong but there's a logic behind the decision.

But with cryptocurrencies there is no underlying asset. Price moves are driven by sentiment alone. When a sell-off begins – and the reason could be something as apparently divorced from the market as the war in Ukraine – it can snowball into a rapid and steep decline. The same is true when values rise.

So what can cryptocurrency actually do for you? Well, exchanges will provide you with a debit card that enables you to buy goods in the real world using your cryptocurrency of choice. But, in reality, most people treat their digital coins as investment assets.

Is cryptocurrency safe?

And that raises the question. Is cryptocurrency a good investment asset class? Put more bluntly, is it safe?

Personally, I don't like crypto. What we are talking about is a relatively new industry that still has an element of the Wild West about it.

Here's what worries me. As things stand no one really knows the direction that cryptocurrencies will take, particularly in terms of their investment potential.

If you look at other forms of investment assets – such as shares and property – there is a history to draw upon. Certainly, there have been times when the share markets have tanked. Equally, we've seen both boom and bust in the property markets of the world on multiple occasions. And, of course, people have lost money.

But these are markets with longevity. There will be good times and bad times ahead – of that I have no doubt – but people will still be buying and selling shares, property and a host of other well-established assets for years, probably centuries to come. What's more, we are talking about investment in very tangible assets – profitmaking companies, bricks and mortar (or glass, concrete and steel). There is also a wealth of knowledge about how markets operate, which in turn means that even novices can access good advice.

It's also important to stress that the traditional financial services industry – the gateway to investment – is well regulated. There are protections in place.

The same cannot be said of cryptocurrency. Will blockchain-enabled digital coins still be a thing in ten years' time? Do financial advisers truly understand the market and its dynamics? Are the majority crypto exchanges financially stable? At this stage, I simply don't know, and neither, I think, does anyone else.

The question I always like to ask is about barriers to entry. Crypto has a very low barrier to entry and I often like to move in the opposite direction to the masses.

Fear of missing out

Even today, after a sharp decline in value, bitcoins are not cheap to buy. Unless you understand the factors that drive the value of the currency, then you are essentially investing in the dark.

So why are people rushing in? Well, there is, in my view, a FOMO (fear of missing out) element at work here. If you read about people who have amassed a small fortune by investing in a digital currency, it's tempting to want a piece of the action. The source of temptation might be a newspaper article, but more likely it's a specialist publication or a YouTube video extolling the virtues of a particular currency or investment strategy.

There's also a range of options for the would-be investor. If bitcoins are falling, other digital currencies may be rising. Thus, a fall in the bitcoin market is not necessarily a deterrent. You will hear about other opportunities.

The hunger for returns opens the door to fraud. An example would be the so-called rug pull scam. These take a number of forms, but here is a typical example. Digital currency platforms also facilitate the creation of tokens linked to the value of a particular coin. These can also be traded and their value rises and falls accordingly. The scammers encourage investment in a low-value token. Using aggressive marketing, they hype the asset and its potential to rise in value. Essentially, victims are encouraged to buy into the currency. When the value hits a certain level, the scammers sell all their own tokens, cashing in at a high price. However, that sale pushes down the token value. The victims who invested are left with assets that are almost worthless. It's essentially a version of the kind of 'pump and dump' scheme that you sometimes see on share markets.

Another source of temptation is the kind of lifestyle video that you often see on social media, particularly YouTube. You may well have seen them. A crypto trader shoots a video in a luxury home, complete with a view of the Caribbean (other seascapes are available) and private pool. For just a few hours a day spent trading cryptocurrencies, all this can be yours, *if* you sign up for an online training course. This sort of thing isn't unique to crypto. You can find share traders, currency traders, and importers and exporters presenting similar videos.

Now these are not necessarily scams. Many will be legitimate. But in the case of the newly minted cryptocurrency market you have to ask if all those experts offering training or simply advice actually know what they are talking about. Are they credible? It's genuinely hard to tell.

Now maybe it's easier to make that call if you are yourself an experienced investor. Perhaps you've already invested directly or indirectly in shares, property or small companies. You know how much money you are prepared to commit and how much you can afford to lose. You also know a bit about the fundamentals of investment – principles that can be applied to different kinds of assets.

But there are people who are being drawn into cryptocurrencies who have done none of these things. They are investment novices. They wouldn't be permitted to put cash into a venture capital fund (which is risky) and they might not even have considered something a little bit unexciting like a cash ISA or a unit trust. But they are prepared to take a chance on a hugely volatile and actually quite confusing market.

They can do this because there is a very low bar to entry. I would suggest that, if you've never invested before, cryptocurrency is something you should be very, very careful about.

Sooner or later, there will be much tighter regulation of cryptocurrencies and their exchanges. That may make it safer, but we could also see the development of a more mature market in which it becomes less possible to make big profits or sustain damaging losses.

To sum up, my advice would be to tread carefully and stay clear of the market altogether if you have no investment experience. If you really do want to get into crypto, check out the exchange you use as thoroughly as possible.

Taking on tokens

There is, however, one by-product of the blockchain/cryptocurrency universe that I feel more positive towards – tokens.

In the cryptocurrency world, blockchain platforms are created to host digital coins such as bitcoin, but that's not the end of the story. Crypto platforms can also create so-called tokens, which also have a value and, like their sibling currencies, can be traded. Some of them are investible.

You may have heard of non-fungible tokens (NFTs) over the past year or two thanks to the role they play in the digital art market. But in addition to NFTs, there are a range of tokens fulfilling different functions.

So what are we talking about exactly? Well, a token differs from a cryptocurrency in that it cannot be used to buy and sell other goods. So while you might use bitcoin as a unit of currency to buy components from a factory in China, you can't do that with a token – at least not directly.

But what the creator of a blockchain can do is assign certain attributes to it. For instance, one of the earliest uses of tokens was to help companies – usually in the tech sector – raise money to develop products. It worked like this: a tech company needed cash to develop a software app and would sell tokens to cover the development costs. Once the software was up and running, those holding tokens would have the right to use the software.

Tokens could also be issued instead of shares, giving the buyers certain rights or privileges. Like shares, tokens could be traded on exchanges.

More recently, it's NFTs that have been making headlines. The acronym NFT stands for non-fungible token. Put as simply as possible, the term 'non-fungible' means the token can't be broken down into components or sold without permission.

That has proved very useful for artists and extremely tempting for investors in digital art. An NFT can be sold in the format of a digital artwork or a piece of music. Because the token is non-fungible, it can't be copied, or if it is, it won't be considered to be the genuine article. Thus, the owner possesses the only genuine copy. It's like buying a physical artwork by Picasso or Van Gogh. As the buyer, you have an original work that others can't own. And because it is scarce, it has value.

For instance, in 2020 an artwork by the American digital artist Beeple (Michael Joseph Winkelmann) sold for $69 million when minted in the format of an NFT. Since then companies such as Bored Ape Yacht Club have also commanded high sums of money.

As with cryptocurrency, there is an important health warning. All art represents a high-risk investment in itself. A painter who is hot today might fall out of fashion. That could be the case whether you buy a physical piece or a digital creation. The added risk is that NFTs will themselves go out of fashion, causing valuations to fall. It's an unknown.

But NFTs have a few more tricks up their sleeve. They can be sold purely as visual or audio works. But NFT tokens can also provide access to a range of services or benefits.

It works like this. When an NFT is sold it comes with an embedded smart contract. A trendy brand could sell its logo or a digital rendition of one of its products for a small fee or give it away for free as a gift. The token could also provide access to special events, such as product launches or a loyalty scheme. These are known as utility NFTs.

It can be a great marketing tool. For example, Wrangler Jeans commissioned pictures of singer Leon Bridges demonstrating his dance moves. For their money, buyers got digital NFTs, physical copies of the pictures and also special access to a New York Fashion Week where Bridges was on hand to meet and greet.

Does this represent a good investment opportunity? Well, it's possible. Digital-only artwork is being sold by brands and artists, and some of it may achieve long-term collectors' item status.

If the logo – or any piece of artwork – becomes particularly popular, the original buyer can resell it, perhaps for a profit. And if not, smart contracts mean there may be other benefits. Buying a high-ticket artwork may be very risky. Buying virtual trainers in the form of a utility NFT from Nike is less of a gamble and it might hold its value. If it doesn't, it's a fun purchase.

Over the next few years, we're probably going to hear a lot more about NFTs, not least because the internet – the natural home for the buying and selling of digital assets – is changing.

Web3 on the horizon

That's because there are two big developments on the horizon. The first of these is Web3. Now, in the geological strata of the internet, Web1 was the era in which we surfed the web, absorbed content and communicated mainly by email or through chatrooms. Web2 designates the era of social media and user-generated content – a period of the web's development that has been dominated both by big tech (Meta, Google, Amazon, etc.) and conventional e-commerce models enabled by bank cards and payment providers such as PayPal.

According to pundits, Web3 will see a web where commerce is underpinned by the blockchain and linked to others using the same technology. That will pave the way for NFTs to be bought and sold seamlessly, both as assets such as digital art or gaming avatars and as a means to access services.

And if Mark Zuckerberg has his way, this will be accelerated by the arrival of the metaverse, a virtual three-dimensional world in which we can interact with each other's avatars. If it comes to pass, it's a world in which we will attend business meetings, go to concerts, spend an afternoon shopping or simply hang out without physically leaving our homes. It's also a world in which cryptocurrencies and NFTs will drive commerce. In this 3D immersive world, we might want to clothe ourselves with digital wearables that we buy in shops and from so-called billboards – essentially interactive shopping opportunities within the metaverse. In this brave new internet world, the blockchain, cryptocurrencies and tokens will become mainstream.

That's the theory. Whether Mark Zuckerberg manages to pull this off is open to question. Cryptocurrencies and tokens will continue to play a part in commerce, but as things stand now, view any investment opportunities with caution and do your homework.

The Rich Forever checklist

- Are you an experienced investor? If not, think twice about investing in cryptocurrencies.
- If you are going to invest, remember the risks. Only invest what you can afford to lose.
- When you make profits, cash at least some of them in to protect your original investment.
- Carry out due diligence on cryptocurrency exchanges. Try to ascertain if they are well run.
- Check the credentials of gurus offering advice on social media. Ask yourself whether the person giving you the information is qualified and reputable enough to do so.
- Decide whether to store your own digital coins or leave them in a wallet managed by an exchange. The former will protect you in the event of an exchange going bust and having all its assets frozen. However, self-storage means you can lose coins if you can't access your system.

CHAPTER TEN
Smart Accounting

How much thought have you given to the work of accountants? Unless, like me, you run a business or have complex financial affairs, maybe you don't think of them very much at all. According to American businessman Aubrey McClendon, 'I just wanted to be a businessman, and to me, the best way to understand business was to be an accountant.' That is certainly one way, the other way is of course to have a close relationship with your accountant to optimise your financial future. In the UK alone, there are more than 500,000 accountants providing services to businesses and individuals. For many of us, their services are vital. And as you increase your wealth, there's an increasing likelihood that you will turn to an accountant for help with your financial affairs. In my experience, the expertise they offer can be invaluable in helping you to grow, manage and preserve your money.

But here's the thing. If you own a business, you definitely need an accountant to ensure the financial side of things is being managed efficiently. If you go to work and draw a salary, on the other hand, you might assume you have no need for accountancy services. Well, that might well be the case, but let's say you're already at the stage of investing across a range of assets. An accountant can certainly advise you on how to manage your money tax efficiently. More generally we can all apply the principles of accounting to our day-to-day money management.

Whether you are running a business or looking after a personal and household budget, there are common rules of the road. Money comes in. Money goes out. The relationship between those inflows and outflows dictates how much cash you have at any given time. The cash that you retain directly affects your resilience in the face of changing circumstances. Equally important, having money available also makes it easier to take advantage of opportunities. And of course, you want to ensure that everything is done as tax efficiently as possible.

So, even if you don't directly require the services of a money professional, it is well worth looking at your finances through the prism of accountancy good practice.

When do you need an accountant?

If you're planning to start a business, it's a good idea to seek advice from an accountant right at the very start of the process.

There are a number of reasons why you should. First and foremost, an accountant will help you to operate tax efficiently from the outset. Even at the earliest stages, you will have options. You can start a business as a sole trader – essentially you are simply an individual engaged in an enterprise that generates taxable revenue. Alternatively, the business could be established as a limited company, operating under different tax rules. An accountant will provide guidance on the best – and most tax-efficient – business structure for your circumstances.

Equally importantly, an accountant will also ensure everything is set up properly in terms of recordkeeping.

Appropriate structures and practices help the business to be tax compliant. That means not only declaring all income and paying the required amount to the state, but also paying only what you need to. No more, no less.

Tax is charged at percentage rates, but there are various ways in which business owners and traders can reduce their annual tax bills. These range from the illegal to the wholly compliant with a few grey areas in between.

So what are we talking about here?

The right and wrong way to reduce tax

Well, there is **tax evasion.** This is a term describing illegal means used by businesses and individuals to pay as little tax as humanly possible. Tax evasion could be as simple as earning £100,000 a year in cash transactions and failing to tell tax officials or hiding money that isn't declared. In other words, tax evasion is a kind of fraud.

Tax avoidance, on the other hand, is not in itself illegal but it can get you into trouble. To take an example, an individual might commit money to a scheme that has been set up to enable its investors to reduce their tax bills. Typically, this scheme will take advantage of loopholes in the tax system.

Now, governments introduce tax incentives to drive behaviour – such as investments in small companies – and these can be used to bring down tax bills in a completely legitimate way. But the tax system has loopholes and anomalies that enable accountants and lawyers to come up with clever tax avoidance measures that were never intended to exist. Tax avoidance schemes are often challenged by the tax authorities. If they are found to be non-compliant with not only the letter but also the spirit of the regulations, there can be back payments and fines.

Technically, the term 'tax avoidance' can also be applied to poor recordkeeping. Again, there is a risk that back payments will be demanded and if information has been left out deliberately, there could also be demand for penalty payments.

Tax mitigation refers to legal, above-board and regulation-compliant strategies to reduce tax bills. For instance, a tax bill can be reduced by claiming for business expenses. An individual can reduce his or her tax liability by investing in approved tax-efficient savings and pension schemes.

Let's assume for a moment that you have no intention of undertaking any kind of tax evasion. That's great. You're a law-abiding citizen. However, without expert help from a professional, the lines between tax avoidance and mitigation might seem a bit blurred. Is that investment scheme something the tax authorities would approve of or could it be challenged? Are all the business expenses legitimate?

More fundamentally, is your annual tax return accurate and free of inadvertent or deliberate mistakes?

These are all questions that an accountant can help you to answer.

Choose your accountant with care

I would argue that the cost of hiring an accountant is money well spent if your circumstances warrant it. But a word of caution.

Tax avoidance schemes were devised by lawyers and accountants. Sometimes, money professionals push the envelope too far. Either they devise and market schemes they know to be non-compliant or they simply get the law wrong.

It's also worth remembering that not all accountants are honest. For instance, former Police singer and long-standing solo rock artist Sting famously took his accountant Keith Moore to court, alleging he had siphoned $9.8 million into close to a hundred banks. Moore was found guilty and sentenced to six years in prison.

In other cases, a settlement is reached. Rhianna sued her accountant and received a $10 million settlement.

Such cases tend to make it onto TV and into national newspapers, but the truth is that even a very quick online search of local newspapers reveals dozens of cases in which accountants have been accused or found guilty of fraud, usually involving wealthy but not necessarily well-known clients. Accountants occupy a position of trust, and very few will take advantage of the access they have to their clients' financial affairs.

As with all financial dealings, it's important to do a certain amount of due diligence when hiring an accountant. Check their qualifications and, if you can, use your social network to find someone that other people in your circle use and trust. There are no guarantees of honesty but you can also help yourself by keeping a close check on your own finances rather than simply trusting a third party. Sting was criticized for not noticing that considerable amounts of money were being siphoned away, although that didn't affect the guilty verdict bestowed on his adviser.

There are some other points to consider. Some accountants specialize in certain industries, such as entertainment. Others provide a range of additional services, such as management consultancy. Pick the one that seems best for you. And remember, human chemistry is involved. The relationship between you and your accountant will be better if you see eye-to-eye on the management of your financial affairs.

An efficient mindset

With that health warning out of the way, let's have a look at some of the advantages of working with an accountant. Or, to put it another way, what are the benefits and how do they justify the costs?

Well, right from the outset an accountant will never be slow to nudge you towards managing your financial affairs in the best possible way.

Andrea L. Richards is a management accountant and founder of Accounts Navigator Associates. Her company's client list includes entrepreneurs, entertainers, tradespeople and investors. Her range of services includes bookkeeping, payroll, management accounting and tax management. We spoke to her about the frontline experience of dealing with clients' financial affairs.

Keep every receipt

As she explains, her first piece of advice to new clients is simple. 'Keep every receipt,' she says. 'If you keep your receipts, we can work into your accounts.'

Andrea's advice on receipts is primarily about the taxes you pay when you go into business. Companies are taxed not on their revenues (the money that comes from clients) but on profits.

Profits are calculated on the basis of revenue minus costs. In addition to staff salaries, costs include obvious components, such as rent (or mortgage repayments), heat, light and telecoms, but anything that is 'exclusively and wholly' used by or needed for the business can be charged as an expense and deducted from revenues to arrive at a figure for profit.

The key phrase here is 'wholly and exclusively'. If you're a tradesperson and you need overalls to do your job, the cost can be charged as a business expense. If, however, you wear a suit to work, the tax authorities – and, to some extent, this depends on the rules specific to jurisdiction – are unlikely to allow it. That's because a suit has a utility that goes beyond work. You can wear it to weddings, funerals and social events. There are exceptions. Entertainers include anything they wear exclusively on stage – even a suit – on their expenses list.

You can, however, charge for meals and hotels. Let's say you're on a road trip to see clients. You may be staying in hotels and eating out all the time. This is essential for the job so the cost of the meal is a business expense. Be aware, though, that tax authorities have their own guidelines on these matters and it's easy to make mistakes. For instance, in the UK, while it's fine to record working meals for you and your staff as expenses, you can't do the same if you've spent money on entertaining a client.

If you employ people, staff salaries and benefits are clearly a cost to the business. And the good news is that staff parties are tax deductible, within certain limits.

Don't forget travel costs. You can deduct the cost of train and air tickets and car mileage when travelling for work purposes. You can't, however, deduct, the cost of the car itself, unless it is exclusively used by the business. Technically, that means it should be kept at the premises, rather than driven home and used to do the school run.

A home office is tax deductible, even if you also have a business premises. But this is a bit trickier, as components such as heat, light and telecoms are difficult to separate from the overall cost of running a home. There are formulae for this. The overall household costs can be divided by the number of rooms in the building, with the number of hours spent working also factored in. Again, an accountant can help you get the formula right.

In addition, businesses can set items such as the cost of office equipment, including PCs, against tax. This is actually a different category. Everyday business expenses are for ephemeral goods and services. You buy photocopier paper and, once used, it's gone. You don't use the same electricity units or telecoms minutes twice.

Equipment, on the other hand, has a lasting value. The PCs and photocopiers you buy are assets. This affects the way they are treated by the tax authorities. You can deduct the cost of relatively low-value goods such as laptops in a single year. More expensive assets often have to be accounted for over a longer period of, with their depreciation taken into account.

A business can also invest in assets that will appreciate in value. These include property, shares in other companies and even art. If sold at a profit, these are factored into the company tax bill.

Keeping receipts for everything can be a bit of pain, but these days there are tools to help you. These include accountancy apps that allow you to photograph a receipt on your phone, which is then uploaded into the accounts software.

So why do you need an accountant to tell you all this? Well, arguably you don't. If you are familiar with the rules of your tax authority and meticulous when it comes to keeping records, then it's quite possible to operate tax efficiently under your own steam. That said, an accountant's expertise will increase the likelihood of you filing accurate and timely tax returns.

Top tax-deductible items

- office expenses
- premises expenses
- remuneration and benefits
- travel
- motor vehicles.

Dedicated bank accounts

Good practice is not just about the records you keep, it's also important to maintain accounts-friendly bank arrangements.

Many sole traders start to earn money before they have really thought about the essential aspects of business life, such as book-keeping. So some payments from customers go into personal current/checking accounts. Others go into dedicated business accounts. Essentials for the office are bought on personal credit cards. Travel is paid for on a personal debit card while meals are secured for through the company Visa or Mastercard.

The result is an accounting mishmash. If you're a sole trader, it's not illegal or even non-compliant; it just makes things more difficult. Any audit by the taxman will take longer because there are multiple personal and business accounts involved. Perhaps more importantly, the accountant will also take longer to prepare your annual tax return and, sadly, that may cost more. Andrea's advice is to be as neat and tidy as possible.

Think ahead. A lack of pressure to file accounts can lull you into a false sense of security. To take the UK as an example, once you've registered as self-employed, your first tax return for, say, the financial year running from April 2023 to April 2024 won't be required until 31 January 2025. But the day of reckoning will surely come. So keep consistent records, rather than attempting to compile everything at the last minute.

The regulatory environment is changing. Technology is enabling authorities to ask for tax information to be submitted every month, rather than once a year. In Britain, this already applies to the value added tax (VAT) on sales and is about to be extended to income tax for traders earning over a certain amount.

It's also worth remembering that, in addition to paying the bill for the previous tax year, the tax authority may ask a sole trader for an estimated payment to cover the current year. So it's vital to have money available to cover tax obligations when they fall due.

Andrea's advice is to set aside a certain amount every month – typically 20 per cent – by moving money by direct debit from the business's current (checking) account into a savings account. 'My top tip would be this – always open a savings account and a business account,' she says.

Efficient transactions

While we're on the subject of bank accounts and cards, it's worth taking a look at how your business can keep costs down by choosing the right mode of payment. If we're talking about day-to-day spending for the business – for example buying petrol or train tickets to take you to meetings – Andrea recommends using a business credit card.

Why? Well, depending on the bank, you might be charged for current account transactions. The more transactions you conduct, the higher the bank charges. The alternative is to use your credit card for everything then pay the bill at the end of the month. That will result in just one transaction on the current account.

Company structure

Businesses can be structured in a number of ways. If you work on your own, the most obvious approach is to register as self-employed. Once that's been done, the tax authority will require you to fill in a tax return every year until the business closes. In the eyes of the tax authorities, you are the business and the business is you.

Under that arrangement – known in the UK as sole trader status – you pay the same rate of tax as someone who is in paid employment. This is straightforward but it may not be tax efficient.

There is, however, another alternative. You can set up a limited company. If you do this, the business itself will be a distinct entity. This opens up a number of possibilities around how you, as an individual, and the business itself are taxed.

Think of it this way. A limited company – and it might have one employee or a thousand – trades goods or services and generates money in much the same way as a self-employed person. But the money earned is taxed at different points. If the limited company employs people, everyone on the payroll will pay income tax. In the UK, both the employee and the employer pay an additional tax known as National Insurance. It's important to pay this second charge as it builds entitlement to a state pension later in life.

The company itself – as a separate entity – pays tax on its profits. Meanwhile, its owners and shareholders can opt to take money out of the company in the form of dividends. These are taxed but at a rate lower than income tax. There are strict rules around dividends. They must be paid from retained profits made by the business. Any payments must be officially declared and minuted.

So, what does this mean in terms of tax efficiency? Well, as a director of a limited company, you can be paid a salary as an employee and also receive dividends as an owner. In addition, the business will be taxed on profits. The regulations will differ from jurisdiction to jurisdiction so, if you're reading this outside the UK, you will need to check the rules as they apply in your country. However, in principle, it may well be financially advantageous to establish a limited company.

It won't be for everyone, but Andrea says that self-employed people with relatively high incomes should look at ways to make themselves more tax efficient. 'I would suggest that anyone with a business making profits of more than £35,000 should consider setting up a limited company,' she says.

So let's assume for a moment that the limited company has one owner/director. The idea is to structure the remuneration as tax-efficiently as possible. This might mean taking a small salary, regular dividends and, of course, paying the corporate tax.

But why take a salary and dividend payments? Well, a salary is useful, not least because it provides a regular income every month while also – ultimately – reducing the corporation tax bill. That's because paying a salary of, say, £12,000 reduces profits by the same amount.

And at that kind of level, there's potentially another advantage. In the UK, no one starts paying income tax until they are earning a certain amount of money, currently £12,570. This is called the personal tax allowance. It's meant to rise every year with inflation, although sometimes it doesn't. If a director is paid below the personal allowance threshold, no tax is payable. However, National Insurance contributions – which rack up state pension credits – are required. 'So the directors don't pay any tax but maintains a state pension entitlement,' says Andrea.

£12,000 doesn't sound like a lot of money, but most of the director's remuneration will come from dividend payments. They can be paid annually or monthly. However, if you take the latter route, you must be certain there will be sufficient profits to match the dividends. Ideally, the arrangement will result in a lower tax bill overall. However, the equation is complicated so take advice.

Is cash really king?

So, how much money should you take out of the business? This is a question that faces not just directors of limited companies but also self-employed people working as sole traders.

For instance, if you're a sole trader, it may be tempting to spend money as it comes in, adjusting your lifestyle to the cash flowing through your bank account. However, that approach can cause problems if business tails off. Maybe you lose a major customer at a time when others are cutting back on purchases in response to economic conditions. As a business owner, you'll do everything you can to provide good service and retain customers, but there may be times when – through no fault of your own – revenues dip or even plummet. Suddenly, there is little or no cash coming in.

Directors of limited companies can face the same scenario. A decline in income leaves the business exposed. As an owner, there will be less money for you to live off – so your lifestyle will be affected – but there may also be a raft of fixed costs to pay and, in many cases, staff wages.

So it's a good idea to set money aside, not just to pay taxes, but to weather any economic or commercial storms. Some businesses grow consistently, others maintain a stable income, but most will encounter difficult times at some stage in their development. Money in the bank is therefore reassuring.

It's also important to maintain positive cash flow. Businesses often fail not because they don't have customers, but because a gap opens up between money flowing in and cash rushing out. For instance, let's say you supply finished goods to a range of customers and give them all a month to pay. Creating the goods involves upfront cost – staff, raw materials, energy, etc. – but the revenue generated might not come in for several months. As a result, there can be times funds run low or dry up.

Hence the expression 'cash is king'. Building up a cash pile helps ensure the business remains resilient in the face of adversity. Putting aside a proportion of profits will help. And if you invoice clients, tight credit control – otherwise known as making sure they pay on time – is an essential part of staying cash positive.

There are, however, other factors to consider. Above a certain level, it might not always be a good idea to let cash pile up in the bank for a rainy day. For one thing, low interest rates coupled with high inflation will result in the value of your money being eroded over time.

Then there's the question of what the cash is actually doing. If it's simply sitting in a bank, the answer is: not very much at all. At least some of it could be spent taking advantage of opportunities that will help make the business more profitable. You might, for example, want to take on an extra member of staff or invest in the development of a new product line. You could even buy property as an investment.

So there will be times when it is right to spend. From her accountant's perspective, Andrea acknowledged the importance of investing in opportunity, but stresses it is important to have the cash available. 'You need cash to take advantage of opportunities,' she says.

There is, of course, another alternative, namely borrowing. That's how a lot of companies pay for their financial growth, and it's not a bad way to do it. There are numerous forms of credit available, including bank loans, overdrafts and invoice finance. The last isn't widely known, but it enables businesses to borrow money against the value of invoices sent to clients. This means the business benefits from cash coming in immediately when an invoice is raised, rather than having to wait for a month or two for the debt to be honoured. All of these can be used to support the business.

But there is, says Andrea, a golden rule: 'If you borrow money, make sure the benefit is more than the cost of the debt,' she says. 'If you are not making money, a loan will be pointless.'

There may, of course, be a judgement call to be made. In many cases, a business owner will be borrowing today to pave the way for tomorrow's revenues. Will those revenues materialize? You can never be sure. What you can do is plan carefully to give yourself the greatest chance of succeeding before you borrow money. That usually requires a business plan with sensible projections coupled with best- and worst-case scenarios.

Looking after staff

Aside from the possible tax advantages, many entrepreneurs choose limited company status because they plan to take on staff. And that's a good thing. If you're operating as a one-man/woman band, essentially you're doing everything yourself. Marketing, administration, product creation, producing work for clients – it's all done by you. By taking on people, you benefit from the division of labour. This enables work to be done more efficiently. You can do more work, sell increased numbers of products and make higher profits.

But staff are both a benefit and a cost. Once there are people on the payroll, there is a wage bill at the end of each month. Again, having a good relationship with cashflow will help you meet your financial commitments to workers as will having a bit extra in the bank for those months when revenues aren't quite so good. But making payroll can be tough at times.

Tough but necessary. 'What you absolutely have to do is look after your workers,' says Andrea.

But what if you need people to do the work but can't afford to employ anyone? Or what if rising inflation and increased pay demands are working together to make it more difficult to meet the cost of keeping your people on board? That has been a particular problem for businesses in recent times. In the period after the COVID pandemic, thousands of workers disappeared from the workforce. Some retired. Others started their own businesses. Some simply found a way to recalibrate their lives, perhaps by agreeing that a two-income household would drop down to one. This trend, dubbed the Great Resignation, has caused labour shortages.

This, in turn, has pushed wages higher, fuelled by demand for workers outstripping supply. Added to that, employers have faced higher energy costs, in no small part because of Russia's invasion of Ukraine in 2022.

So, as an employer, how do you cope? One answer is to take advantage of the growing freelance workforce. There have always been freelancers available to employers, but thanks to the internet – and, to be more precise, freelancer market sites – it has become easier to manage supply and demand.

One of the advantages of using a freelancer is tax efficiency. True freelancers look after their own tax affairs. The employer doesn't have to worry about paying any additional taxes – such as National Insurance in the UK. Nor is there any pressure to provide additional benefits – medical insurance being a case in point. Freelancers tend to be paid for hours they work, or the projects they are involved with and nothing more.

However, there is a growing pushback against employers who take on 'full time' freelancers. For instance, a recent UK court case found that Uber drivers were not freelancers in the accepted sense. The judge ruled they were entitled to workers' rights, such as paid holidays. It's important to check the rules in the jurisdiction within which you operate.

In the case of full-time workers, it's worth checking out the opportunities to reduce the tax bills of both the employee and the employer through 'salary sacrifice' schemes. In the UK, it works like this: an employee agrees to sacrifice a proportion of salary in return for a non-cash benefit that nonetheless has a value.

In practice, this could mean the employee will receive childcare vouchers, gym membership and health insurance in addition to a pension. Pay is docked from the worker's salary to pay for the benefit, but that also means they pay less tax. In the UK, the employer also saves on National Insurance payments.

For larger companies, there can be a significant tax saving. More importantly, such schemes are thought to help retain employees without paying them more. The success of any salary sacrifice initiative revolves around providing individual workers with benefits they genuinely value.

The rise of the side hustle

Not all businesses are full-time ventures. You might make some money through a so-called side-hustle, a small business that earns cash on top of your salary or pension.

Again, the internet has played an important role in promoting the popularity of side hustles. Witness the Airbnb revolution. By signing up to a website, anyone can rent out a room, apartment or house. The key to this is an online market connecting the buyer and the seller. A holidaymaker seeking a room in Paris. A commuter looking for a cost-effective place to park. A homeowner in search of power tools for hire.

Equally, the internet has provided a means to market side-hustle activities. For instance, you can use social media coupled with a Shopify-style e-commerce website to sell pottery. You can sell courses through a range of sites.

Not all of these businesses will grow to generate enough income to live on – although many do grow and thrive – but they provide something extra.

A small amount of income won't trouble the tax authorities very much. For instance, here in the UK, you don't have to file a return for anything less that £1,000 a year. But above a certain limit, a tax return will be required. Again, the principles we talked about earlier apply. Keep good records of earnings and expenses.

Money management for everyone

This book is not being written exclusively – or indeed primarily – for entrepreneurs or the self-employed. It is intended for everyone who wants to manage money more efficiently. And as Andrea stresses, there are things that we all can do to put themselves in a better financial situation.

'The first thing I would say to everyone is clear your debts,' she says. 'Clear the high-interest rate debts first and work from there. And when you've cleared your debts, start saving.'

Andrea is also adamant that everyone should be saving for a pension. 'I'm a big advocate of pensions,' she says.

The pensions landscape has changed considerably over the last two decades or so. In the past, a great many occupational pension schemes (those provided by employers) provided a guaranteed income as a percentage of final salary. What that percentage actually was depended on the employee's length of service. These were known as defined benefits, or final salary, plans.

They tended to be most common in the public sector but they were also offered by large private sector businesses such as car companies. Sadly, they are rare today. In an age where people are living longer, employers feel they are unaffordable.

Instead, most people are signed up to a defined contribution pension. The employee makes a contribution every month – as does the employer if it's an occupational scheme. The money is invested, building up a pot in the form of shares and bonds. On retirement, the value of the investment is realized with a cash value. The employee can take a percentage of the pot as a lump sum and the rest buys an annuity. This means the money is reinvested and there is a contract with the insurer or pension provider. You invest your pot of money. The insurer guarantees you an income for as long as you live.

There is no capital gains tax to pay when you realize the value of your pension, and once converted to an annuity the income is paid monthly. There are perhaps some risks – or at least things to look out for. The value of the pension pot (before conversion to an annuity) is linked to the performance of the share and bond markets. Retiring when the market is depressed can affect your pension income. Potentially there is a danger that some catastrophe will happen in the financial service industry, leaving people with worthless pensions after a lifetime of savings. Andrea doesn't think that will happen. 'Pensions have been with us for a long time. They work,' she says.

The more you contribute to a defined contribution scheme, the more you receive. In addition to an occupational scheme, you can take out top-up pensions. You can make your own investment decisions if you open a SIPP (self-invested personal pension).

In the UK, employees opt into an occupational pension by default when they join a company. It is possible to opt out. Andrea doesn't recommend this. A pension is a good tax-efficient long-term investment.

There are other tax-efficient ways to invest. Broadly speaking, the returns made on an investment – and that could be profits from a wallet loaded with bitcoins, a property deal or money realized from a shares portfolio – incur a capital gains tax (CGT) charge. The amount you pay in percentage terms depends on the jurisdiction. For instance, in the USA, taxpayers below a certain income don't pay capital gains. In the UK, there is a capital gains tax allowance. Any gains below the allowance threshold are not subject to CGT. At the time of writing the threshold was set at £12,300, but this is set to fall sharply in coming years to bring in more revenue. As things stand, CGT on profits from a property sale are charged at higher than the normal rate. This doesn't apply if you're selling your own residential property.

There is considerable scope for tax planning. The simplest way is to invest in a CGT-exempt savings plan, such as an ISA in the UK. There may also be tax breaks for investing in start-up and scale-up companies.. However, if you have a range of investments, losses in one asset class can be set against gains in another. You can also use your tax exemption. It doesn't carry over from year to year, so if you're going to sell an asset and ring up a profit, it may make sense to do it in the current financial year, rather than waiting until the next period when you could well have other assets to sell. If you have a range of investments, an accountant will help you be as tax efficient as possible when you take profits.

Not everyone will require an accountant's services, but if you run a business or invest, the perspective of a professional can be a good money-saving investment in itself.

Andrea L. Richards's top accountancy tips

- Get an accountant at the start of your business venture. They will advise you on the most appropriate company structures, recordkeeping and tax efficiency.
- Register with the tax authorities. In Britain, use HMRC online services (accessible through the government gateway).
- Open separate bank accounts for each business.

- Raise invoices as soon as work is completed. This cuts down the time between finishing the work and payment by the customer.
- Record receipts, at least monthly.
- Keep bank statements and receipts for at least six years.
- Remember your home office costs are tax deductible.
- As a director pay yourself a minimum wage. This is deductible from profits.
- Use a registered office and not your home address.

The Rich Forever checklist

- If you are starting a business, find an accountant who can provide the range of services you require.
- Get into good habits from day one. Maintain good records and keep all receipts.
- Make sure your business is structured in the appropriate way. In many cases, registering as a limited company will be more tax efficient.
- Ensure that you are paying what you owe in tax. Not a penny more, not a penny less. An accountant can provide advice on what is tax deductible.
- Apply the same principles to your personal finances. Take advantage of legal tax breaks and thresholds to minimize your tax burden.
- Regularly set aside money to pay your tax liabilities.

CHAPTER ELEVEN
Guarding Your Wealth

Very few people actively enjoy purchasing insurance. In contrast to the instant gratification of buying the car you've always wanted or the arguably more profound sense of achievement when money transfers from one bank account to another and you find yourself in possession of a dream home, buying the associated insurance is something we have to do but which doesn't trigger the pleasure centres of the brain.

But what it does provide is a sense of security, as insurance broker Ella Weinberg says 'Insurance doesn't create generational wealth, it avoids generational consequences.' If that car is stolen, the insurer has your back. If the worst happens and your house burns down, you still have somewhere to live and the money to purchase a new property. Likewise, we insure our phones, pets, household goods and possibly a whole host of other things, knowing that insurance protects us from the consequences of unseen events.

But many people – although they may not think about it – are underinsured when it comes to protecting themselves and their families against the financial impact of illness or death.

Think of it this way. Your house is obviously a hugely important asset, but if you're paying off a mortgage then the continuing ownership of the property depends on your ability to honour the mortgage payments. If you can't maintain an income, there is a real risk of the property being repossessed.

The wider point here is that you are actually your own greatest asset. You generate the income that pays for everything you have. So what happens in the case of ill health? Who makes the payments and, equally important, who takes care of any dependants?

Ill health is usually a short-term consideration. The majority of problems are resolved in a few weeks or months. But even a relatively short period of sickness can throw an individual's finances into disarray over a much longer period – perhaps even over a lifetime.

And, sadly, ill health can also end in death. Again, the same questions arise. What happens to those who are left behind? Will they have the money they need, not just to survive comfortably but also to maintain the lives they have become accustomed to?

Ella Weinberg is an award-winning insurance broker and financial consultant trading as Ella Ensures. As she puts it, the case for using insurance to protect the financial wellbeing of individuals and their loved ones is cut and dried. 'Insurance', she says, 'is a means to sustain the lifestyle we live, go on paying necessary direct debits, fund the rearing of children, and protect the ownership of assets. Unless these things are protected other consequences follow. Credit scores fall, generational wealth is eroded, and a business suffers. Your legacy suffers.'

If you run a business, the chances are that the ability of you and your team to work effectively is crucial to its continued success, so it is important to think about how it can be protected should some kind of catastrophe strike. For instance, a key member of staff falling ill – it could be you or someone with a particular essential skill – could disrupt activity to the extent that revenues and profits fall sharply. Again, insurance products can provide the protection required to navigate a path through unforeseen challenges.

So the good news is that you can protect yourself, your loved ones and your business by choosing the right insurance policies (I'll be looking at the options later in this chapter) but that's not the end of the story. You also need to ensure that your money and assets are managed well in the event of illness, accident or death. That means thinking about making a will and also arranging for someone to look after your affairs when you are unable to.

Insuring your life and health

But let's start with insurance. The range of products available today is bewildering. Frankly, there is not much that you can't insure.

So what are the policies that everyone should have in order to protect themselves and their loved ones?

Health cover is increasingly an essential purchase. The primary purpose of this kind of policy is to provide healthcare when it is needed. The principle is simple. You pay a certain amount of money every month and this provides access to treatments ranging from physiotherapy to surgery. Typically, a policy will include hospital treatment, consultations, access to GPs (general practitioners) and physio. Policies can also cover mental health treatment.

For many people reading this book, health insurance will be a fact of life. For instance, in many countries – notably the USA – insurance payments represent the only way to secure healthcare when required without facing an enormous bill. The policies may be taken out by individuals or provided by employers as a benefit, but the principle is the same.

The situation in the UK, where we are based, is different. The UK has a tax-funded National Health Service (NHS) that is free at the point of use. Nevertheless, many people chose to take out additional healthcare.

Now, at this point, you might be asking why I'm including health insurance in a book about generating and preserving wealth. The answer is simple. Good healthcare – and that starts with prevention – is essential to preserving wealth. If you are chronically ill – or, to put it another way, suffering from an illness that persists over years – you're unlikely to be performing at your absolute best. That will affect your income. A serious illness – no matter how short-term – may prevent you from working at all.

So it's important to know – and be assured – that all the necessary treatment will be available as and when required. That's why a lot of people in the UK choose to take out health insurance. As good as the National Health Service is, it faces huge pressures. So much so that waiting lists for certain treatments can run into many months or years, and when pressures on the system build, cancellations are common. Private healthcare insurance enables policyholders to sidestep the waiting lists and access treatment quickly. And the faster you're cured, the quicker you can return to focusing on career and revenue generation.

The cost of health insurance depends on a number of factors. Prices are based on age, postcode and available health facilities in your area, with the scope of the required cover factored in. It can be bought for an individual, a family or, in the case of a business owner, as part of an employee benefits package. If you run a business, cover through the company can be filed as a business expense. You can choose a premium to match your budget and circumstances.

Income protection

While health insurance ensures you get the treatment you need while avoiding unnecessary delays and without drawing on savings, it can't guarantee your ability to work. 'You may have to take time off over a long period because of back trouble or stress,' says Ella. 'If you aren't in a position to work because you are too sick, then it becomes difficult to pay everyday bills.'

This is a particularly acute problem for the self-employed. Put simply, if you are too sick to work, you won't be in a position to generate income through your own efforts and customer payments into your bank account will – sooner or later – dry up. But even if you are employed, your income may still be at risk. The sickness benefits provided by employers (usually in the form of paid leave) are limited. Beyond a certain point, payments will stop. Long-term illnesses can seriously damage your financial wellbeing.

An income protection plan will provide regular monthly payments for the period when you are unable to work. The minimum claim period is typically 12 months with the maximum being the lifetime of the policy.

Income protection – as the name implies – is linked to your earnings. It will pay a percentage – up to a maximum of 70 per cent – of your salary for the duration of your illness. For those who are self-employed or whose earnings can fluctuate, there are policies available where the pay-out can be fixed at the outset of the cover, thus ensuring you always receive the maximum percentage of income, even in a year where you may have earned less. As Ella points out: 'An income protection policy means you won't have to borrow money or deplete savings and you can avoid missing crucial payments. You can sustain your lifestyle and continue to afford necessities.'

At the point of claim, the insurer will require evidence of your current income. That's fairly easy if you are an employee – you can simply provide the insurer with payslips for the period in question. If you are self-employed, the insurer is likely to ask for evidence in the form of tax records for a given period. However, there are policies designed for self-employed individuals where providing proof of earnings can be difficult and so a fixed pay-out can be secured. Only evidence of the illness is necessary,

Life and critical illness cover

Critical illness insurance exists to fill in the financial gap that can open up if a serious health problem impacts you in any way.

Critical illness policies pay out a lump sum when the policyholder is diagnosed with a serious medical condition. The money can be used as the recipient sees fit, but is usually to pay hospital bills, fund adaptations to their life or simply support the family at a difficult time.

In many respects, this is similar to life insurance cover and the two can be sold as a package. But there is a crucial difference. Life insurance – which also pays a lump sum – is triggered by death. And in terms of the wellbeing of loved ones, it is essential.

'Anything that needs to be paid for after you have passed away needs insurance,' says Ella. 'Typically, that means children, a business, or assets such as property. You have to ask yourself who is going to pay for these things, if you are not here.'

Life cover is extremely reliable. For instance, Aviva, one of the UK's biggest providers pays out on 99 per cent of claims. This is pretty much the industry standard.

Premiums are based on age, BMI and smoker status. And while you can take out a policy for as little as £5 a month (this figure will vary according to jurisdiction), insurers will always recommend discussing the cover with an adviser to guarantee you are adequately insured. This can be anywhere up to ten times your annual salary in the event of death.

The amount of cover you require is a very personal decision. We're not here to advise you on that, but there are some things you should take into consideration. For instance, when you look to the future, what level of financial support will your family need? Breaking that down, what sort of costs will they face in terms of mortgage payments, household bills, school fees, debts, funerals and so on? From there, you can work with an adviser to decide on an appropriate level of cover.

There is no limit to the amount of life cover that can be purchased. However, if an individual seeks to ensure his or her life for a very large sum, the insurer will undertake a financial or medical assessment.

There is also the question of when you need to purchase it. Ella says that cover should start as early as the point at which you enter a career. It will become critical at the time when you enter into commitments such as mortgages and having children.

Life and critical illness cover can be bought in a combined package or as separate components, possibly from different insurers. There can be benefits associated with splitting the cover or having it all in one place, and it's probably a good idea to seek help, but a client will always have control over what they purchase. Many policies cannot be sold without an adviser including income protection.

That's actually quite an extensive menu of cover and not everyone will feel they want to commit to multiple monthly direct debits. It's a question of priorities. Ella says that everyone should have income protection. 'And anyone with children should have life insurance.'

Essential business insurance

If you run a business – either as a director of a limited company or as a sole trader – you are probably keenly aware that some forms of insurance are absolutely essential. Often, these are to protect the business from claims made by customers, members of the public or staff. These include:

Public liability policies are designed to protect against compensation claims made by members of the public who interact with the business. For instance, if a visitor to a hairdressing salon has an accident on the premises and makes a claim, public liability insurance can provide the funds to pay compensation. **Employee liability insurance** plays a similar role, should a member of staff claim against the company.

Many business owners will also take out **professional indemnity policies.** If you provide a service and make some kind of a mistake, you can be exposed to legal action. For instance, let's say you run a business that provides marketing material for clients in the form of brochures or web pages. If the document contains intellectual property (IP) – such as a photograph – that isn't cleared for reproduction, your customer may be sued by the owner of the IP. That customer may then seek to recover the loss from you. Professional indemnity insurance can help mitigate your own losses by covering legal fees and compensation payments.

Then there is **business interruption insurance**. This provides financial support when a company is forced to temporarily cease operations because of some kind of adversity. For example, a fire or a flood could halt operations for days or weeks, causing a sharp downturn in income.

And these days there are new threats. A malicious piece of software downloaded onto an office computer network might bring all operations to a standstill. To take an example, the software could lock all the files and the attacker will then demand a ransom to free up the system. The alternative is to purge all the computers of the malicious code, a process that could take days or weeks. Thus, it makes sense to have insurance for any income gaps caused by disruption.

Product liability cover kicks in if a customer suffers damage caused by a faulty or badly made product and decides to sue.

Stock insurance covers the cost of replacing goods in the event of fire, flood or theft. And, of course, it's important to protect premises through **buildings and contents insurance**.

Beyond the basics – key person protection

Those are the basics, but one form of insurance is often overlooked. Right at the beginning of this chapter, I pointed out that you are your own greatest asset. You have value in terms of skills and earning power.

So let's apply that principle to a business environment. In an ideal world, if a manager, owner or member of staff needs to take time off – say to recover from an illness – there should be someone else to step in.

But we don't always live in an ideal world. For instance, start-up businesses are often built around one of the founders. It could be that they are great at selling or managing the team. Founders can be reluctant to delegate – although this tends to change as businesses grow or seek investment – so either by accident or design they become key to the whole operation. To a greater or lesser extent, the business relies on their expertise and talents. Their absence can create real problems.

The same can be true of other members of staff. A start-up technology company might rely on the 'genius' of one or two software coders. A restaurant's reputation may be dependent on a particularly talented chef. A B2B company might have been built on the efforts of a well-connected, trusted and persuasive sales director.

And always the same question applies: how does the business cope when this key player is, for whatever reason, out of action? The answer lies in finding someone to come in – perhaps on a temporary basis – with matching skills. That's fair enough, but that talented individual has to be paid for, possibly at a time when profits and/or revenues might have taken a dip.

That's where key person insurance comes into play.

There are two options here. Key person income protection pays out a monthly benefit, should an important member of staff fall ill or sustain a serious injury. As with personal income protection, the amount paid is contingent on the reward package of the individual with salary and dividends factored in. The monthly payments go to the company rather than the individual.

A second option mirrors the kind of lump sum payment protection you get with either a life or critical illness policy. However, it is tailored to the needs of a business rather than an individual. Just as you can insure your own life to provide a lump sum to your family in the event of death or serious sickness, a company can do the same thing. Again, the lump sum paid by the insurer goes to the business rather than to any individual. The company can then use that money to mitigate the loss of a vitally important member of staff.

That second kind of key person policy pays out in response to three scenarios, namely death, a terminal illness or critical illness. What that last scenario means in practice will be down to the policyholder and the insurer. Normally, the nature of the critical illness covered will be spelled out in the policy.

In both cases, the money paid out by insurers can be spent entirely at the discretion of the company that has taken out the policy. To take some practical examples, the money might be used to offset any slide in profits or fill in the gap left by a delay in raising cash through a bank loan or an equity investment. Equally, it could be used to fund the search for a replacement and any necessary training.

It's important to stress that critical illness cover is applicable to sickness only. For instance, it won't protect the business against the costs of a team member being away on maternity leave. However, if there was a complication with a pregnancy that resulted in illness, that could be covered, depending on the terms and conditions of the policy.

Any company can take out key person insurance. Arguably, it is smaller businesses that tend to benefit most, for the simple reason they tend to have a smaller pool of human capital to draw on should an important member of the team die or fall ill. But the truth is that much larger companies can also find themselves dependent on those few individuals who are capable of making a difference.

So when might a business decide to take out key person insurance? Well, it's a case of looking at the payroll as it stands now. Are there members of that team whose absence would genuinely impact – in a bad way – revenues or operations? The list could include some obvious candidates – the founder, sales director and head of operations perhaps but you might cast the net a little wider. For instance, is the finance director crucial to raising investment or securing loans? And are the marketing director's overseas contacts likely to play a vital role in any planned expansion into other territories?

Once the crucial people have been identified, a company might decide to take out a policy on several members of staff. They won't themselves benefit from the cover, but buying a policy on their behalf will, nonetheless, require their permission. The same people might also want to take out critical illness cover.

Another useful policy for businesses is relevant life. This is life or critical illness cover, booked through the business – and is therefore tax efficient – with the money paid out to the relatives of employees in the event of death. It can also be purchased on behalf of the business owner and provides further protection.

Where there's a will ...

So far we've been looking at insurance as a wealth management or, to be more precise, wealth protection tool.

But while insurance on its own provides cash in the event of a medical or personal crisis, it will not necessarily define who receives the money.

Most people who take out life insurance know who they want the money to go to – a partner and children being the most likely beneficiaries. You can put life insurance into a trust to ensure the pay-out goes to the right person. But if an individual dies without leaving a will, the question of how the rest of their estate (cash and assets) is divided up can become a lot more complicated,

A will is, therefore, vital. 'It is essential in terms of expressing your wishes after you have passed away,' says Ella.

Without a will

The exact details will vary according to which country you live in, but broadly speaking if an individual dies without a will, there are a number of rules governing inheritance.

Here in the UK, the rules of intestacy (dying without a will) favour the legal partner of the deceased, while there is also some provision for children and grandchildren. In a nutshell, the legal partner (through marriage or civil partnership) inherits everything up to a certain value (£270,000 at the time of writing) and half of any money and assets above that level, with the rest being divided up between any children or grandchildren.

That sounds fair, but it may not reflect the wishes of the deceased. For instance, a divorced former partner has no call on the estate.

By the same token, if a couple have separated but not divorced, the estranged partner stands to inherit, even though the deceased may have been in long-term (but not certified by marriage) relationship with a new partner.

As such, the deceased may be survived by a group of loved ones. Some will stand to inherit. Others won't. To avoid disputes and a drawn-out probate process, write a will.

It's possible that some people are deterred from writing a will by the perceived legal complexity of the process and the cost. In reality, it isn't difficult to find someone to write you a will for a relatively small outlay.

Writing a will

One obvious route is to approach your local solicitor but there are other options. For instance, you can approach a professional will writing company. The latter won't necessarily employ qualified solicitors. That's not necessarily a problem, but you should check their credentials. For instance, are they a member of – and regulated by – a professional will-writing body? In the UK, that would typically be the Society of Will Writers (www.willwriters.com).

In addition, some charities offer will-writing services, and many banks will also help with this aspect of generational wealth planning.

Once written, a will can be stored electronically, physically and/ or with the company that has written it on your behalf. 'There is always a register, so provided someone knows you have a will it can be retrieved,' says Ella.

Writing a will can involve quite a lot of thought, even before you decide on how your estate will be divided.

In addition to money in the bank and property, you will also need to consider the value of your life insurance, investments, and pensions, plus any personal property from works of art and jewellery to musical instruments and furniture. If you run a business, you should think about who inherits it and how it will be managed.

Executors

One key decision is the appointment of an executor.

It's a term that you hear all the time – whether in a movie or TV show where a will is part of the plot – or on the financial advice pages of newspapers and magazines. But unless you've actually got to the point of making a will, the role of an executor and the appointment process may not be something you've ever thought about.

An executor is someone appointed by you to ensure the provisions of your will are all honoured. The role can be assumed by one person or several – in the UK up to four – but often there is a primary and secondary executor to split the workload.

Whoever assumes the role is taking on a big responsibility. Thus executors should be people you trust.

And that could mean taking a long hard look at whether a potential executor might have some sort of vested interest that potentially runs counter to the interests of the other beneficiaries. Ella uses the example of a single parent with an estranged partner. In one sense, that partner might be an ideal choice to ensure the children from the relationship receive their inheritance. From another perspective, the partner could be absolutely the wrong choice. It's a question of deciding who you trust.

Equally, they should feel comfortable doing the job.

Anyone can be an executor as no formal qualifications are required. You might appoint a trusted friend or a family member, and the executor can also be a beneficiary of the will. On the other hand, an executor can also be professional, such as a solicitor or someone supplied or suggested by a will writing service, if you have used one. The important thing is that the people you choose should be available when you need them. Thus, if you select a professional, there should be a recurring relationship. 'That's really to ensure that you don't lose contact with them,' says Ella.

Some will writers will also be executors. Typically, they will charge for this service, perhaps taking a percentage of the assets. Ella suggests that this is only appropriate if you would otherwise struggle to find a suitable executor.

The first task of an executor is to locate the will document, so they should be fully informed about its whereabouts. Once they have it in their hands, they have two tasks: making sure the terms of the will are adhered to and managing your estate. The latter could mean ensuring that all debts are paid and closing down bank accounts. They may also have to sell assets to split the money up between beneficiaries.

If there are significant assets, the executor may also have to apply for probate. This is another of those terms that is 'out there' but often little understood. In a nutshell, it is the legal process under which a will is confirmed as valid. It comes into play when there are significant assets, such as property or shares that must be sold.

In other words, being an executor is a time-consuming task that requires commitment. Not everyone – perhaps especially close friends or relatives – will be happy to assume the role so soon after losing someone they love, so it can make sense to select a professional.

It is possible to put assets such as property and cash into trusts. For instance, you might set up a parental trust to ensure that your assets are managed on behalf of your children until they come of age. Or you could establish a property trust to manage a portfolio of assets on behalf of the beneficiaries. This would require the appointment of trustees.

Under UK law, trusts come in a number of forms, including:

- absolute
- split
- discretionary.

In the case of an **absolute trust**, all the named beneficiaries have a right to the assets contained within the trust.

Discretionary trusts, on the other hand, allow the trustees to make certain decisions about how money and assets will be used and distributed on behalf of the beneficiaries.

Split trusts provide a flexible arrangement. Policyholders can use the trust to assign certain insurance benefits – such as the pay-out from a life policy – to beneficiaries while keeping others for themselves. For instance, critical illness cover payments could be assigned to the policyholder. It is well worth seeking advice on the most appropriate trust arrangement.

Power of attorney

An executor manages your affairs after you die. Sometimes, however, it makes sense to appoint someone who can manage your financial and legal affairs when you are very much alive, but perhaps unable to do certain things for yourself.

This is actually quite a common situation. For example, as people get older they often find it difficult to get out to the shops or visit the bank. So, they might ask one of their children, a relative or a friend to do their banking.

In many cases, this kind of arrangement is more about convenience than anything else. The older person may be broadly speaking well but just a little infirm and in need of some help.

In other cases, however, we might be looking at a serious illness that absolutely prevents an individual from carrying out everyday tasks. And this can have very serious consequences. Let's say someone is too ill to manage their own affairs. That illness could prevent them from releasing funds from a bank account that could actually pay for treatment.

In another scenario, an individual might be out of the country for a protracted period of time. During that period, there may be a requirement to sign legal documents or – again – pay bills.

The solution in all these situations is to appoint someone who is legally entitled to act on another person's behalf. This is known as granting power of attorney.

As Ella points out, granting power of attorney is another way of keeping control. 'If something happens to you and you can't manage your own financial affairs, you may feel your long-term partner is the best person on the planet to manage them for you. If you don't hand power of attorney to that person, you won't necessarily be able to make that choice.'

Ordinary and permanent

Power of attorney can be granted either for a limited period or on a permanent basis, depending on the situation.

In practice, someone who is incapacitated but likely to recover, or someone who is travelling overseas with an intention to return, might grant power of attorney for as long as it is necessary. In the UK, this is known as ordinary power of attorney.

Permanent power of attorney comes into play in the event of a situation that is irrecoverable. Usually, that means a loss of mental capacity because of an illness such as dementia. It may also be appropriate in the case of serious physical incapacity.

Power of attorney can be granted over a complete spectrum of financial affairs – such as buying and selling property, managing bank accounts or settling debts. The arrangement may also cover management of lifestyle and health issues. Or it can be limited to specific functions.

There is a legal process to go through. The process is simplest when the person granting power of attorney still has mental capacity. It simply involves completing forms and then registering the arrangement with the appropriate authority. The exact process will depend on the jurisdiction.

Again, it's important to choose someone you trust to manage your affairs because whoever takes on the role will have a huge amount of power to act on your behalf. Assuming you can find that person, then the power of attorney – rather like writing a will and appointing an executor – will provide a means to ensure that your affairs are well managed and your own interests looked after, along with the long-term interests of your dependants.

There's a tendency that many of us – perhaps all of us – have to avoid thinking about some of the real calamities that life can throw at us. That in turn can deter us from putting in place measures to mitigate the financial impact of sickness or death. But no one can expect to get through life without some kind of health crisis or accident. To take an example, according to statistics, one in two people can expect to have some sort of a brush with cancer during their lifetime. We all know death is inevitable but it's tempting to see it as a far-distant event. That isn't always the case. As such it is important to have written a will and have the right insurances in place to protect yourself and your family.

Ella Weinberg's top tips on insurance

- If you are serious about creating wealth, then you should be serious about preserving it. Insurance is essential to sustaining a lifestyle and protecting wealth in the event of serious illness or death.
- Anything that must be paid for after you have passed away needs insurance. Top priorities include children and businesses.
- A wide range of cover is available but, at the very least, everyone should have income protection, and if you have children, life insurance is absolutely essential
- A will is essential to ensure that your wishes are carried out in the event of death. It is a way of expressing your wishes.
- Consider granting power of attorney to a trusted third party. There can be serious consequences if something happens to you and you can't manage your financial affairs. Granting power of attorney is another way of keeping control.

The Rich Forever checklist

- Assess your personal and family insurance needs. In addition to car, home, content, pet and gadget insurance, it's important to think about the consequences should you die or fall seriously ill. If you have a family, will they be able to pay the bills if you are no longer able to provide an income?
- Consider life insurance, critical illness cover, income protection and health insurance.
- Insure your business. In addition to public liability, employee liability, product liability, business interruption, buildings and contents cover, there are a range of policies that help the business to survive if you or key members of staff are incapacitated. Key person insurance is particularly important to protect the business if an essential member of staff dies or becomes seriously ill.
- Write a will and appoint executors
- Consider granting power of attorney to someone you trust.

CHAPTER TWELVE
Generational Wealth and Legacy

The expression 'born with a silver spoon in your mouth' used to be applied as an insult. The implication was that any wealth or success enjoyed by the subject of the verbal jab was simply inherited rather than being a product of talent or hard work.

But times have changed. Parents have always wanted to pass wealth on to their children. Just as Jay-Z expressed in his song 'Legacy', 'Generational wealth, that's the key. My parents ain't have sh*t so that shift started with me.' In the past, that might have been the privilege of an elite few, leaving the majority of the population to look on as, in a relatively small number of families, money and assets cascaded from one generation to the next. But today what we're seeing is much more accumulated wealth around than ever before. Consequently, increasing numbers of people have a significant legacy to pass on to their loved ones.

This represents a genuine generational shift. Even today you can look around at the stories of countless people who have succeeded in business or enjoyed stellar careers despite – or perhaps because of – a tough start. If asked the question 'What did your parents leave you in their wills?' they are likely to say 'nothing' or 'very little'.

Success changes the game. The accumulation of money and valuable assets allows all of us to enjoy a great life and also give our children and grandchildren the best possible start. An inheritance could make a huge difference to the lives of the next generation. Why wouldn't you want to do that?

So the 'silver spoon in mouth' insult has lost its sting. More people enjoying a good start in life is the goal that arguably we should all be working towards.

And, ideally, that initial transfer of wealth from one generation to the next should be just the start of a story. You help your children, they in turn leave a legacy for their own children, and so on it goes. Wealth snowballs. As Beyoncé famously puts it in her song 'Boss': 'My great-great-grandchildren are already rich, that's a lot of brown children on your Forbes List.'

Making and losing – the generational wealth cycle

That's the theory. In practice, things aren't quite so straightforward. Creating a legacy is about more than passing on wealth. It is also about taking steps to ensure that money and assets earned through hard work and talent are preserved and built upon by the generations that come after.

And that can't be taken for granted. A 20-year survey by the Williams Group found that 70 per cent of families lose their wealth by the second generation and 90 per cent by the third.

You can see wealth as a mountain: there is a path up and a path down. The path up is about making it. On the other side, the path down sees the wealth disappearing. The accumulated wealth of one or two generations becomes diluted over time rather than replenished.

There's a quotation that has gone viral on the internet in recent years that illustrates the point: 'My grandfather walked ten miles to work every day, my father walked five. I drive a Cadillac. My son is in a Mercedes. My grandson will drive a Ferrari but my great-grandson will be walking again.'

Originally coined by G. Michael Hopf in a science fiction novel, it has since been deployed by financial experts and motivational speakers as a simple way of summing up what is often a cycle of generational wealth and how it comes and goes.

And the novel provides an explanation, too: 'Hard times create strong men. Strong men create good times. Good times create weak men. Weak men create hard times.'

It's a neat analysis of how wealth comes and goes, but does it hold true? Hopf was writing a novel, after all, not an economic essay.

How the Medicis lost their wealth

Well, witness the fate of the Medici family. If you've ever been to the Tuscany region of Italy, you've probably come into contact with the Medici legacy, perhaps without even knowing it. They were a banking family who spread their wings to also become a political dynasty. Their wealth was vast, and you can see the echoes of it today in the palaces they built and the art they commissioned.

Somewhere along the line, they lost most of it. Over time, children and grandchildren managed the banking business poorly. Rivals not only made the most of the opportunity but also contrived to strip the Medicis of their political influence. There was a dynasty there, but it didn't last forever.

You can see similar if less dramatic stories closer to the modern era. The Rothschilds were also a hugely wealthy banking family. They can trace the origins of the family back to the 15th century, but the banking empire began to take root 300 years later with Mayer Amschel Rothschild in the driving seat. Today, although the family is still worth around $400–$500 billion – depending on where you glean your statistics – they are no longer in the top echelon of rich families. In fact, they are ranked in the 160s.

Now, they are not exactly short of cash, but the story illustrates that, over time, family money can dilute and dissolve.

So what exactly happens? How do people fuck it up?

Well, there's lottery winner's syndrome to consider. A large amount of lottery cash is handed to someone with little money management experience. Huge sums disappear, sometimes because of reckless spending but very often as a result of poor investment. Similarly, a large inheritance will certainly be welcomed by the recipients but they won't necessarily have the tools, knowledge and talent to build on that legacy and transfer similar sums to their children. Thus, the road to sustained family wealth becomes a dead end.

The dilution of wealth can also be down to a lack of motivation. We live in an age of relative abundance. There are many opportunities to make money and ultimately become wealthy. But it does only require not talent and knowledge but also a willingness to work hard for a goal. That requires motivation. People who acquire wealth without any generational legacy behind them are often driven by the ever-present awareness that nothing can be taken for granted. Wealth comes but it also goes. You have to work hard to retain it. And when wealth is passed on to children, memories of hard times or even poverty are within the living memory of the family, which is a motivational factor.

That driver doesn't necessarily exist for grandchildren and great-grandchildren. They are born into relative affluence. Some will take their good fortune entirely for granted and fail to acquire the skills and knowledge necessary to build on what has gone before.

Education matters

That's not always the case. Some families succeed over many generations because parents make a point of educating their children and talking to them about money.

This isn't necessarily an easy thing to do. First of all, there are cultural considerations. In the UK, it's often said that people are fairly reluctant to talk directly about money. That's probably a bit of a stereotype but it is one with a strong element of truth. Certainly, that's something we've experienced.

The reticence about discussing money matters is not confined to the workplace or social occasions; it is also seen within families. Even very successful parents won't necessarily educate their children about money matters. There are consequences. One or two generations down the line, there is very little awareness about what it took to create the wealth that is enjoyed by the family.

There may also be a talent issue. Just because you're a successful business owner or have carved out a career in a high-paying profession, it doesn't necessarily follow that future generations will either be good at the same things or feel any strong desire to pursue the same goals.

No parent can dictate to children what they should or should not do with their lives. A family's wealth might be based on running a business. The next generation could pursue law or medicine. Their children could be aspiring novelists or artists. People do their own thing.

But what parents certainly can do is provide as much knowledge as possible, first and foremost by talking to their children about how money works. It might even be a good idea to include the younger generations – children and grandchildren – in some of the decision making around the family finances – say around property deals or share transactions.

This kind of open communication will help the rising generations make better decisions in their own right and thus help them manage the wealth they will ultimately inherit.

Financial education

It's also important to encourage good financial habits. One simple example – and this is something we recommend strongly – would be showing your children how to build and maintain a good credit rating. This will make it easier to access credit at good rates but there are benefits as well. Almost by definition, having a top rating goes hand in hand with good financial habits: paying bills on time, using credit wisely, and budgeting properly, rather than putting everything on the card and watching the debt levels rise.

It's also a good idea to help your children buy their own properties as soon as possible. That doesn't mean they have to be tied down to one spot. If their primary aim is to travel the world or get international career experience by working abroad, the property can be rented out to provide income while also growing in value as an asset. This provides an early example of borrowing money to grow wealth. And here's the really great thing. Part of your legacy is delivered when you're alive. You can see your children buying assets and enhancing their own lives.

You might also consider a custodial account. Essentially, this is a bank savings account opened by an adult for someone below the age of 21. In the purest sense, these accounts are designed as sources of finance through which securities such as shares can be bought and sold. Crucially, the transactions have to be managed by the responsible adult.

In practice, these accounts enable experienced adults to show their children how investments are made and why. Once control of the account is passed on at the age of, say, 21, the holder is well versed in financial matters.

More fundamentally, parents can teach the value of money, even when children are very young – for instance, by making it clear that everything has value. One way of doing this is to place limits on toys and other gifts, even if the money is available to buy everything the child might want at any given time.

Types of wealth

Wealth takes many forms. First of all, there is personal wealth – essentially, the assets and money accrued by individuals. This is often in the form of money, property or investments such as stocks and shares.

Personal wealth is often relatively liquid – or, to put it another way, accessible when you need it. Shares can be sold. Money can be withdrawn from the bank. Even the value of a property can be realized in a fairly short period of time.

So personal wealth can be left in a simple and straightforward way to the next generation. There are some choices to be made. For instance, if you have rental property – and we believe everyone should have at least two houses or apartments rented to others – it can be sold. But it can also be passed on to provide children or grandchildren with an income, underpinned by an asset that appreciates. This kind of passive income has been a theme in this book. We believe it's an important aspect of building wealth.

Then there's family wealth. This doesn't tend to be so liquid. For instance, properties and businesses might be left in trust and managed as income-generating assets to benefit the wider family or named individuals.

Some thought needs to be given to the future of these family assets. For instance, who looks after the business? Are you providing the right education to children who might one day be looking after the day-to-day running of the company themselves?

Making plans

Planning is, therefore, essential. And yes, planning can be boring – especially if you're looking ahead to a time when you won't be around. But if you don't plan, you increase the risk that your children and grandchildren won't benefit fully from their legacy.

So have you made plans for after your death? If you haven't, now is a good time to start.

Generational wealth planning checklist

- When devising a generational wealth strategy, it's important to ask yourself the following:
- What does generational wealth mean to you? This is personal for everyone and depends to some degree on financial circumstances.
- What will you be passing on to future generations in terms of money and other assets?
- What do you want that legacy to achieve? This a key question. Rather than simply passing on wealth because you can, you can play a part in shaping the lives of future generations by crafting your legacy.

If you have very little in the way of money, assets or personal possessions, you might nevertheless want to pass on something: a few thousand pounds in cash, jewellery, personal items that will mean something to those who survive you. What you have may well be split among several people, with the inheritance personalized for each one.

It won't be life-changing for the legatee, but it will mean a lot.

But let's assume for a moment that your net worth exceeds a few thousand pounds in the bank and some personal possessions. You have one or more properties, shares, significant savings, and a business. Now you have an opportunity to make a real difference to the lives of those who come after you. But what does that mean? Money to buy a house? Help with university costs? Take some time to think about your goals.

Or you could be more ambitious. You could be looking at providing your children and grandchildren not just with a great start but also an opportunity to really change the game. Perhaps you didn't start with much, but your hard work provides the foundation for generations of family members who won't have to struggle – people who are comfortable with and knowledgeable about money; people who know how to earn money, make it grow, spend it and pass it on.

This represents real transformation.

How much can you give?

One important question is how much can you give? The average legacy is about £60,000, which in today's money is not a lot. It's similar in the USA, were the average legacy is $46,000. Again not a huge sum. But the headline data is slightly misleading. So-called baby boomers – born in the first couple of decades after World War II are sitting on billions of pounds' or dollars' worth of money and assets. But there is a big gap between the wealthiest and those who have little to pass on – hence the low average.

In that respect, £60,000 or $46,000 shouldn't be seen as the benchmark. The more you can accumulate, the greater the legacy for the coming generations.

This raises a question:

How can you move into the zone in which you can pass on something that is transformational? What are the steps?

One thing you can do straight away is to take out a life insurance policy. This is pretty much a no-brainer. The cost to the individual can be as little as £2.00 a week for cover in the region of £200,000. That's a significant sum that will be paid out on your death. The more you set aside each month, the higher the pay-out will be.

In the first instance, it might go to your spouse rather than children or grandchildren, but importantly it's money that either stays in the family as a lump sum and perhaps a source of investment cash. Even if it is used to pay bills, mortgages and school fees, it is indirectly preserving wealth.

Investing in property

Then there is property. A single residential property is a hugely valuable asset to pass on, especially in towns and cities where prices are high. For instance, in London, the average house price is more than £500,000. In some parts of the city, you could pass on houses that would turn your children into overnight millionaires.

So if property is a good thing, why not consider buying more than one? If the deposit money is available, taking out a mortgage to purchase a house or apartment to rent to others is fairly straightforward. The rental income pays the mortgage, plus a profit on top. In addition, history suggests the value of the property will rise significantly over time.

What you can then pass on to your children is an asset that can be sold or retained to deliver passive income.

There are other ways to benefit from property. For example, you can invest in publicly traded investment companies that own and manage properties – in the UK, these are known as real estate investment trusts (REITs). Put simply, investing in a REIT is a little like buying shares, but the returns will come from a portfolio of properties.

Stocks and shares

Shares can be a safe investment, providing a greater return than a bank savings account. The easiest way to get exposure to the stock market is through a managed fund which tracks major indices, such as the FTSE 100. Some funds offer higher returns but inevitably the risk of the investment losing value is higher.

Another approach is to actively pick stocks with the potential to gain in value. In Chapter 6 on the stock market, we talk to Debodun Osekita who is on his way to creating a pension pot worth £1 million from an investment of £5,000. His pot currently sits at £50,000 after six years of investment.

Passing on a business

One of the most effective ways to build wealth is to grow a successful business. There are two approaches to this. One could be described as 'build and sell'. This is the strategy of many entrepreneurs. Their goal is to create a venture that has sufficient traction in the market to attract potential buyers. Many founders don't take much in salary when they have ownership because their goal is to sell for a life-changing sum of money.

At the other end of the spectrum are businesses where the founder has no desire to sell. Instead, the aim is to create a venture that will provide a good income over a lifetime. These often become family businesses, passed down through generations.

Companies evolve. You might start as a sole trader, expand to take on a few employees and then enjoy further growth from there. There is a point when the business becomes an entity in its own right. That's often the stage at which the founder (or founders) are no longer integral to success. The owner-manager has been replaced by a CEO from the outside. The business has a life of its own. It is no longer dependent on a charismatic founder. Instead, it has a brand.

The founder may step back to let his or her children take over. Alternatively, the business could be managed by a CEO (and a team of directors) recruited from the outside. It's a good idea to set up a limited company. Under this arrangement shares can be allocated to your children. If they choose to take a back seat and outsource the management to others, they still enjoy a passive income. The important thing is, there is now a brand that will endure.

There are some potential pitfalls. Let's say you plan to pass on the running of the business to one or more of your children – quite a common ambition. Communication between the generations is important. For instance, if you are handing the baton to several children, there may need to be a certain amount of negotiation about the roles they'll take on and whether or not they will be comfortable doing so. Even if the plan is that one person will take the helm, there may actually be very little interest. Bianca's father was keen that she should be involved in his kitchens business. She really had no interest in kitchens.

And what if the business is managed by outsiders. Again, there should be discussions about the role that those who inherit might play in determining the direction of the company.

There is a bigger point here about communication. It can be really uncomfortable to talk about your own death and what happens afterwards, but the generations really should work together on the planning.

Top family businesses

Think Dell or Rolls-Royce – family names synonymous with the businesses that carry their names. The same can be said of Walmart (a derivation of Sam Walton). Then, of course, there are businesses such as Volkswagen and Chanel (owned by the Wertheimers for three generations) that are family owned without revealing that information in the trading name.

Top ten family businesses (*source:* EY and University of St Gallen)

1 Walmart
2 Berkshire Hathaway
3 Cargill Inc.
4 Schwarz Group
5 Ford Motor Company

6 BMW
7 Koch
8 Comcast
9 Dell
10 Reliance Industries

Diversification

It's worth thinking about the asset you intend to leave to those who survive you. Active investment often involves quite a lot of risk, especially when you are seeking higher returns.

That's absolutely fine when investing on your own behalf, but once you start looking to the future, it makes sense to think about investments that will stand the test of time. For instance, you might want to have some gold in your portfolio (see Chapter 8). Prices fluctuate, but the historical evidence suggests the precious metal holds its value over time. At I write, prices are sitting close to a ten-year high.

Property is also a good bet. It's a simple equation. There is only so much land available and this limits the scope for building. At the same time, populations are growing. The rules of supply and demand suggest that the trend in the property market will continue to point upward. Land Registry figures show that UK prices have increased by 70 per cent in the last ten years.

There are no guarantees and prices do rise and fall across all asset classes. However, by diversifying you can hedge the risk. This plays an important part of effective legacy planning.

Keeping track of your assets

Diversification is a good thing, but it can also make life more difficult for those who survive you unless you have provided a clear map of the assets you own and where they can be found.

When Bianca's grandfather passed away, he had savings in various bank accounts and we didn't know how to capture everything. That made it much more difficult to carry out the wishes expressed in his will.

And the more you have – perhaps spread across a whole range of business or personal interests – the more important it is to keep track of everything. That could mean current and savings accounts (business and personal), ISAs, a shares portfolio, investments in property deals and also physical assets such as gold or art. So leave instructions.

Ideally, everything should be documented and available – along with your will – to the executors of the estate and, possibly, the tax authorities.

If you don't capture all your assets, your loved ones and other beneficiaries potentially face a struggle. There will probably be some kind of a paper trail that might include bank statements and correspondence (electronic and physical) from financial service providers. Tax returns can also be a useful source of information in terms of tracking down details of income from investments. But this won't necessarily provide a comprehensive picture.

There are some online tools available. In the UK, Mylostaccount.org.uk provides a means to track down accounts. It is operated by the British Bankers' Association, the Building Societies Association and National Savings & Investments. In the USA, Missingmoney.com offers a similar service.

The alternative is to engage the services of an asset recovery company. This won't be necessary if you make a point of keeping good records.

Above all, make a will. If you don't, government agencies will manage your estate. That can be a long-drawn-out process, with no guarantee that your wishes will be respected. Indeed, without a will, no one can definitively know your wishes.

Bianca and I have tried to make things as simple as possible by creating a will that puts everything in trust. That means we don't have to detail everything.

In practice, a whole range of assets can be placed in a trust – often referred to as a revocable living trust – including:

- bank accounts
- share certificates
- shareholders' stocks
- annuities
- certificates of deposit (CDs)
- safe deposit boxes
- personal items.

In addition to capturing the assets you wish to pass on, this kind of trust also has the advantage of speeding up the probate process – under which estates are scrutinized by the tax authorities – which in turn ensures that beneficiaries shouldn't be kept waiting for months or perhaps years.

Divorce

Up until this point, we've been talking about families as if they are one fairly simple unit consisting of parents, children, grandchildren and on down through the generations. In reality, couples get together, marry, divorce and remarry. This clearly complicates legacy planning.

So what happens to the family wealth when partners go their separate ways and other people come into the picture? The fear that some wealthy individuals have is that romantic attachments that lead to marriage and end in divorce result in wealth being diluted.

Hence the growing popularity of pre-nuptial agreements. These essentially define how money and assets will be divided in the event of a split. They are particularly popular in cases where there is a wealth-divide between the two partners.

Are they a good thing? Many people would take the view that marriage is a partnership and that it is only right and proper to split the assets in the event of a divorce. A legal separation need not be fractious, even when large sums are involved. Announcing his divorce from McKenzie Bezos, Amazon founder Jezz Bezos stressed a commitment to continuing as friends. McKenzie received a $% stake in Amazon – at the time said to be worth around $38 billion as part of the settlement. A record sum.

But what if someone marries late to a less wealthy partner who perhaps already has children. If the union rapidly falters, should the latter be entitled to a full divorce settlement with the children from the previous marriage benefitting? Or would the best solution be a pre-nuptial to sort things out in advance? Some would say yes. Others say no – marriage is marriage. Dividing the assets is part of the deal.

We both have our views on it. Ultimately, though, it's something for couples to decide.

Philanthropy

It's worth remembering that your legacy is potentially more than the value of assets bequeathed to children, grandchildren and other relatives. A legacy can also be defined in terms of the people you have helped.

You don't have to die to leave a legacy. The legacy left by philanthropists often begins when they are still very much alive. American industrialist Andrew Carnegie famously said: 'I spent the first half of my life making money and the second half giving it away.' We don't necessarily go along with that as a philosophy, but giving can be very satisfying.

You don't have to be a billionaire or millionaire to support the causes you're passionate about. A great many people bequeath a percentage of their wealth to a charity or cause of their choice. Equally, you can donate regularly during your own lifetime. This has the advantage of being tax efficient.

Equally important, you can donate your experience and skills in support of organizations you care about or simply help people on a one-to-one basis through mentoring or financial support.

Giving back has always been an important part of our journey. Together we have both fundraised for charities, and given our expertise on charity boards or via training. And we continue to have our own social enterprise to help others in their pursuit to build successful businesses or careers via employability skills training.

These can all be part of your legacy.

Minimizing taxes

No one wants to pay more tax than they should. That applies not only if you are filling in a self-assessment form or preparing the accounts for a limited company but also when you are making plans to pass on wealth to coming generations.

So, the golden rule is simply this: you should use the parameters of the law to minimize your tax bill.

In the UK, inheritance tax is charged on the estate of anyone who dies. In practice, that means just about everything that has a cash value – money, property, investment assets, possessions – is subject to tax. The rate of taxation is 40 per cent. So, on the face of it, at least, the revenue authorities can take a serious bite out of the money and assets you've worked so hard to accrue.

In the UK, the threshold at which an estate is taxable is quite low by international standards and currently sits at £325,000 compared with just £250,000 two decades ago. Any cash or assets above that level are subject to tax.

The situation in the USA is markedly different. At the federal level, no one is liable to estate tax unless they are relatively wealthy. At the time of writing the threshold stood at $12.9 million, with the figure being evaluated every year by the Internal Revenue Service (IRS). Thus, very few Americans pay this tax. The headline rate of tax is 40 per cent but there are lower tiers. However, a number of states have their own inheritance tax system. A case in point is New York, where tax rates of between 3 and 16 per cent are charged on estates valued above (at the moment) $6 million.

The country you live in has a major impact on the amount payable to the government. But the principle is the same. Once you climb about a certain level of wealth, inheritance tax is a real concern.

So what can be done? Well, it may not be as bad as it looks.

Sticking with the UK, for a moment, when a married person dies, the estate generally passes to the spouse and there is no inheritance tax to pay at that point. Equally important, the nil-rate band of the deceased passes on to the spouse. This doubles the tax-free ceiling – on current figures pushing it up to £650,000. There are also discounted rates for money and assets passed on to children.

Many people opt to put their assets into trusts. Creating a trust that releases wealth to children over time means that the assets within won't form part of your estate when you die. A trust can be designed to hand over, say, 10 per cent of the total value every year. This not only mitigates the tax payable but also acts as a brake on the recipients blowing their inheritances in one fell swoop. There are a number of types of trust, including absolute, split and discretionary (see Chapter 11). A solicitor or account can advise on the most appropriate to your needs.

Residential property is treated compassionately. If you die and leave your home to your children, the tax-free threshold effectively doubles. This is a recognition that residential property prices are extremely high in UK, and it would therefore be unfair to extract too much tax revenue from something – in the shape of a house or apartment – that is essential for life.

That said, the fact that residential property prices are sky-high means that many people will find that tax is due on their estate, even if the house is the only major asset. You can, however, gift a house to children. There will be no inheritance tax to pay if – and this may be a very big if – you live for a certain number of years (currently seven) after the gift is made.

And actually, the same principle applies to other gifts. Money, property and possessions can all be gifted to children and no tax will be payable as long as you live for seven years. If you don't, there is a sliding scale of tax, based on how long you actually do survive. In addition, small gifts can be made tax-free, as can gifts for weddings for children and grandchildren.

This is undoubtedly a good thing. For one thing, you can minimize the final inheritance tax bill by giving away assets early. On a personal level, doing so means you have the pleasure of seeing your children enjoy some of your wealth. Provided you yourself are not impoverished as a result, this is very satisfying.

Charitable giving is also tax efficient. When more than 10 per cent of an estate's value is donated, the remainder is taxed at a lower rate.

The caveat with tax law is that everything can change quite quickly. But the big-picture message is that careful tax planning makes a real difference to the amount of money available to the next generation. I've outlined some of the exemptions available in the UK, and there will be similar mitigation options in other jurisdictions. But it's a complex area and you may want to take professional advice.

Good tax planning is an important component in the preservation of wealth, which in turn is part of the cycle of making money and passing as much of it as possible on to the next generation.

I hope that we have proven that estate planning is not only for the wealthy: everyone should have a plan.

The Rich Forever checklist

- Decide what generational wealth means to you. What would you like to pass on?
- Teach your children good financial habits. Talk to them about money.
- Build your wealth through investment.
- Plan your legacy.
- Write a will.
- Consider putting assets in a trust.
- Plan to minimize inheritance/estate tax.

A final word

In our previous two books, *Self Made* and *The Business Survival Kit*, we focused on building business growth and the emotional intelligence to not only survive but to thrive. In this book we have provided the trifecta of how to take that knowledge and build a solid financial legacy.

We live in a world where we are in control of our financial freedom: we have something called choice and we want you, by reading this book, to make the choice to not only change your financial position but also the financial position of the generations that come after you.

We wrote this book ...

- for you
- for your family
- for the generations that come after you.

It starts with mindset and ends with application.

We have provided you with all of the tools for you to become successful.

We have used the knowledge and experience of some of our favourite global superstars and experts – and it is evident that we all share the same goal of being rich forever.

If you have found the practical hints and tips in this book inspiring, we encourage you to buy a copy for a loved one and change their financial life and legacy, too.

Share your journey with us on @biancamillerofficial and @mrbselfmade

Contributor Contacts

Thanks again to our expert contributors for sharing their experience and insight.

Accountancy

Andrea L. Richards from Accounts Navigator

Andrea L. Richards is an experienced accountant who has been helping small businesses to optimize their profits and reduce taxes since 2003. With a keen eye for detail and a client-focused approach, Andrea empowers entrepreneurs to achieve financial success and growth.

https://accountsnavigator.com/
info@accountsnavigator.com

Insurance and wealth protection

Ella Weinburg from Ella Ensures

Ella Ensures helps you keep your current money and safeguard future money and gives you access to new money by educating and implementing relevant wealth protection tools.

www.ellaensures.com
hello@ellaensures.com

Property investment

Alfred Dzadey

Alfred Dzadey is a multi-award winning property investor and entrepreneur. He is the Founder and Director of Real Property

Ventures, a prominent property business specializing in affordable, high-specification co-living accommodation in the UK.

Alfred has built a 4-million-pound property portfolio within just three years and raised millions from private investors, showcasing his exceptional business acumen. His achievements include winning the 2021 New Property Investor of the Year award and the 2022 Best Entrepreneur in Real Estate at the Stevie Awards. He was also a finalist for the 2022 Great British Entrepreneur Awards in the category of Young Entrepreneur of the Year in the West Midlands region.

www.realpropertyventures.co.uk
alfred@realpropertyventures.co.uk

Stocks and shares

Debodun Osekita from the Stockpickers Academy

Stock Pickers Academy (SPA) is a 5,000-plus-strong community of both experts and beginners leveraging each other to improve financial literacy and build wealth mainly via the stock market but also through other assets such as property, currencies, commodities, crypto, angel investing in start-ups, and investing in shares of private companies. SPA has partnered up with Finimize and has a range of celebrity clients from music, entertainment and sport. The community also supports entrepreneurs by connecting them with vital expertise as well as investors. Key mantras include 'Investing is for everyone', 'You don't go broke taking profit' and 'Planting trees, not get rich quick'. Members of the community identify as Spartans most of whom have taken the eCourse where the unique SPA strategy is taught in a way suitable for complete beginners, although experienced investors have also testified to gaining invaluable insights.

www.stockpickers.academy
debodun@stockpickers.academy

Glossary

Alternative Investments Investment assets that lie outside the familiar investment classes. Alternative investments can be financial in nature (hedge funds, VC funds, commodities, gold) or tangible goods with the potential to appreciate. The latter group includes watches, art, collectables, high-end consumer goods and wine.

Annualised Percentage rate (APR) The interest charged on a loan over a year.

Base Rate When news bulletins report that central banks have raised interest rates, they usually mean the base rate. The base rate designates the interest charged on commercial loans to banks. When the base rate rises, banks pass this on to borrowers.

Blockchain Blockchain technology – also known as distributed ledger technology – underpins cryptocurrencies. Every time a cryptocurrency is bought or sold, the transaction is logged on an electronic ledger.

Bonds A bond is an investment interest. Essentially it is an IOU agreement under which the bond issuer agrees to repay a debt with interest over a fixed period of years. Bonds – which can be issued by central banks or companies – are tradeable on financial markets. When their prices rise, the yield (interest rate payable). When the price drops, the yield rises.

Buy to Let Mortgage A mortgage advanced to borrowers who plan to buy and rent properties.

Capital Gains tax The tax charged when an asset is sold to a third party. For instance, the sale of a large number of shares would trigger a Capital Gains Tax charge.

Cash Flow　Cash flow is essentially the difference between money coming into a business or a household and the amount flowing out. If more money is earned than spent every month, cash flow is positive. The reverse of that results in negative cash flow.

Company Tax　The tax charged to companies on profits.

Copy Trading and Mirror Trading　A service provided by many share trading apps. Inexperienced investors (and others) can buy and sell shares based on the activity of more experienced traders.

Credit Score (or Credit Rating)　A system used by banks to establish whether borrowers are creditworthy. The score is based largely on payment records and credit usage.

Cryptocurrency　A digital currency created independently of banks and governments. It can be used to buy and sell goods or as an investment asset. Bitcoin is the most famous but there are thousands of others.

Cryptocurrency Exchange　The platform through which cryptocurrencies are traded.

Cryptocurrency Wallet　The storage mechanism for cryptocurrencies. These can be managed by the owner of the currency or a crypto exchange.

Dividends　Payments made by listed and private companies to their shareholders.

Equity　Equity in the context of investment usually refers either to shares held in a company. In the context of property, equity is the amount of the property you own as defined by how much you've repaid on the mortgage plus the value of the deposit.

Exchange Traded Funds　Investment funds usually focused on specific asset classes such as property or commodities. These operate as managed funds – with investors pooling cash – but they can be traded on markets such as the London Stock Exchange.

Gross Domestic Product/Growth　This is the primary mechanism for measuring the health of national and global economies. GDP measures economic output. Rising output means the economy is growing.

HMO A property market term meaning houses in multiple occupation. One property investment strategy is to buy residential houses and convert them into multi-occupancy flats to increase the rental return.

Income and Growth In investment terms, income is revenue generated by assets such as shares are property and paid regularly to the holder. For instance, property generates rental income. Growth defines the rate at which the asset increases in value. When property values rise, that is growth. Similar shares pay regular dividends but may also grow in value.

Income Tax A tax on the income of individuals.

Indices (Stock Market) Indices such as the collect data on listed businesses. For instance, the FTSE-100 index is comprised of Britain's top 100 listed companies. By averaging the performance of each of the member companies, indices provide a measure of performance.

Individual Savings Account (ISA) A tax-free account that can be used to save money or invest in unit trust or individual shares. The nearest US equivalent is an IRE (Individual Retirement Account).

Inflation/deflation A measure of rising or falling prices. Consumer price Inflation is calculated by taking a basket of goods and finding an average of how far their prices have moved since the same month a year earlier. This provides the inflation rate.

Invoice Discounting An arrangement under which businesses borrow against invoices sent to customers. The money is advanced when an invoice is raised, providing the business with instant access to capital. It's a cash flow too.

Key Person Insurance This provides a lump sum or the equivalent of a salary to businesses that lose key personnel due to illness or death.

Leverage Money borrowed to buy an asset that will deliver a return.

Life Insurance   An insurance policy that pays out a lump sum on the death of a named individual. It's also possible to insure against critical illness.

Limited Company   A legal structure used to constitute companies of all sizes. Primarily billed as a vehicle to limit the liability of directors should the company fail, it can be the most tax-efficient vehicle for small business owners.

Liquidity   Liquid investments can be easily converted to cash. For instance, shares can be sold and the profits returned to the seller almost instantly. Some investments, such as property, are not quite so liquid. Assets such as art may be difficult to sell in a set timeframe and are not considered to be particularly liquid.

Managed Fund   Manages a portfolio of assets on behalf of investors.

Power of Attorney   Granting Power of Attorney means giving a trusted third party the right to look after your financial affairs either temporarily or permanently. Should you be incapacitated, a Power of Attorney order should mean your finances will be kept in good order – for instance, bills paid.

Quantitative Easing   A process by which central banks pump money into their economies to stimulate demand.

Recession   Broadly speaking, a recession is a prolonged downturn in economic growth as measured by Gross Domestic Product. More technically, a recession is officially declared if the economy shrinks for two consecutive three-month periods (quarters).

REIT   Real Estate Investment Trust. REIT operators own or manage income-generating real estate, using pooled capital from investors.

Rolling Credit   Credit arrangements where the agreement is ongoing. For instance, a credit card allows continual borrowing for as long as the arrangement lasts. This is the opposite of Fixed Term Credit where the arrangement ends when a loan is paid off after an agreed period.

Secured Debt This is a debt where the lender uses the borrower's assets – often a house – as collateral. If the payments are not made, the lender has a call on the value of the asset.

Sole Trader The simplest means for a one-person-band to go into business. A sole trader registers with the tax authorities and declares revenue and profits at the end of each financial year. The profits are taxed as income. The business is the individual, the individual is the business.

Term Loan A loan that is repayable over a set period of time. The repayments are usually monthly.

Trust A trust is a vehicle for managing money, investment assets and property. All of these can be placed within the trust, which is overseen by trustees. They can provide a tax-efficient way to pass on wealth to coming generations.

Stock and Shares Stocks and shares are almost but not quite the same thing. If you buy shares in a company, you own a proportion of its stock. A share is the smallest unit of ownership.

Unit Trust A Unit Trust is a managed fund. The fund manager invests in a portfolio of assets using capital pooled by investors.

Unsecured Debt Debt that is not secured against an asset such as a house.